The Marquis de Sade

Twayne's World Authors Series
French Literature

David O'Connell, Editor

University of Illinois

TWAS 724

"Imaginary Portrait of the Marquis de Sade" by Man Ray
Photograph courtesy of Sotheby Parke Bernet,
Editorial Photocolor Archives

The Marquis de Sade

By Lawrence W. Lynch

College of Charleston

Twayne Publishers • Boston

The Marquis de Sade

Lawrence W. Lynch

Copyright © 1984 by G. K. Hall & Company
All Rights Reserved
Published by Twayne Publishers
A Division of G. K. Hall & Company
70 Lincoln Street
Boston, Massachusetts 02111

Book Production by Marne B. Sultz

Book Design by Barbara Anderson

Printed on permanent/durable acid-free
paper and bound in the United States of
America.

**Library of Congress Cataloging in
Publication Data**

Lynch, Lawrence W.
    The Marquis de Sade.

    (Twayne's world authors series.
French literature ; TWAS 724)
    Bibliography: p. 144
    Includes index.
    1. Sade, marquis de, 1740–1814—Criticism and interpretation.
I. Title.   II. Series: Twayne's world authors series ; TWAS 724.
III. Series: Twayne's world authors series. French literature.
PQ2063.S3L9 1984   843'.6   83–22748
ISBN 0–8057–6571–9

for Mary C. Lynch,
my wife and best friend

Contents

About the Author

Lawrence W. Lynch is an associate professor of French at the College of Charleston, South Carolina. From 1975 until 1983 he was a member of the faculty at Southeast Missouri State University. He received his Ph.D. from the University of Iowa in 1975. He also studied at the University of Laval and at Middlebury College. He has taught in France as a lecturer in English in Rennes (1968–69) and as an exchange professor at the University of Nancy II (1980).

He is the author of *Eighteenth-Century French Novelists and the Novel* (1979). His articles have appeared in *French Review, Comparative Literature Studies, Kentucky Romance Quarterly,* and other scholarly reviews.

Preface

In conformity with the nature of the Twayne series, this volume is meant to be an introduction to the life, writings, and ideas of the Marquis de Sade. Many know Sade only by reputation, or only from reading one or two of his more salacious books. But to know and appreciate him completely, one should also read his earliest philosophical writings, his short stories, and his conventional works. Consequently, the reader of this volume will find synopses of most of Sade's known works, followed by commentaries and analyses of their main aspects, and a presentation of the various interpretations of them. A large portion of the latter area derives from three principal sources: the exegesis of Sade by Gilbert Lely and Maurice Heine in the first part of this century; a wealth of biographies and literary criticism written on Sade since 1945; and more recently, a growing number of books and articles written primarily by women. Sade always provokes a reaction, accurate or erroneous, for or against. By indicating the basic elements of Sade's own literary production and philosophy, together with the major systems of their interpretation, I feel that the reader should be in a position to formulate his or her own judgments of this author.

The biographical data in the first chapter of this book does not explain all of Sade's works. He was sexually promiscuous, an adulterer, and at times perverse by any definition. He was also a prisoner, confined for most of his adult life at the request of his wife's family. He did not nor could not have practiced all the acts of violence and aggression described in his works. Nor were these writings merely a written protest against confinement: prison afforded him the opportunity to read extensively, to imagine, to copy occasionally, but foremost to create works that are unique to him alone. At times Sade is quite conventional in relation to the philosophical and literary period in which he wrote; his evaluations of other authors can be quite astute, even modern. At other times, he displays personal jealousy, unbridled hatred, and lack of consistency. Sade is frequently accused of repeating himself, as he often does in the expanded versions of his most famous work *Justine* and in his catalog of perversions in *Les 120 Journées de Sodome*. But he also provided posterity with a great diversity of literary form and content which will maintain interest and provoke controversy for years to come.

Cruelty toward women, sodomy, and murder are not ordinarily favorite topics of interest, but these are the subjects which one must confront in any serious discussion of the Marquis de Sade. He is consistent in his belief that immediate and unrestricted sexual gratification is the utmost priority in life, and that the means to this end is a limitless quantity of valueless and faceless victims, usually women, who are completely subordinated to the caprices of their aggressors. Occasionally a female character will assume a position of superiority (for example, Juliette), but the *Justine* pattern of endless submission to persecution is the prevalent one. We cannot expect Sade to have made his beliefs coincide with the women's awareness and freedom movements which came about two centuries after his death. Nor can we completely forgive his abuse of them, albeit in fiction. In defense of Sade, he seemed genuinely sincere when he claimed that by portraying vice with *élans* and "wrapped in the colors of hell," he was contributing to the subsequent avoidance of vice.

Sade is not always pleasant to read, but it is my hope that, after detailing and evaluating the specifics of his works, the conclusions drawn will have a more objective basis than the past categorical accusations of "infamy" and insanity. I do not feel that everyone should in fact read Sade, nor that his books should be present in every school library. If I have not made him more palatable to some, I hope that I have made him more understandable.

A number of people have assisted me in the planning and execution of this project. I wish to express my thanks to Professor David O'Connell for the initial suggestion of writing a book on Sade, and for his continued guidance. I am also grateful to my typist, Jenny Kubinak, for her hours of help in preparing the manuscript. I am particularly indebted to my colleague at Southeast Missouri State University, Professor Charles Hearn, for his faithful reading of each chapter and suggestions concerning style. If any eccentricities of expression remain, they are my responsibility. Mrs. Barbara Nourie was extremely helpful with proofreading the manuscript. My wife also read and helped to edit each chapter, and for her support and encouragement, I dedicate this book to her. Finally, a small regional university is not always equipped with all the resources needed to complete a work of this nature; thus I express my thanks to Mrs. Marybeth Needels for obtaining dozens of items through the inter-library loan service, and to Alan Nourie of Auburn University, for keeping me abreast of new material on Sade, through computerized indexing.

Lawrence W. Lynch

College of Charleston

Chronology

days later by Inspector Marais acting on the orders of Mme. de Montreuil. Begins sixteen months of incarceration in Vincennes.

1778   16 July, after being interrogated in Aix, escapes from his guards; remains at large for thirty-nine days. 26 August, arrested at La Coste by Marais, and spends the next eleven years in Vincennes and the Bastille.

1782   Completes *Dialogue entre un prêtre et un moribond.*

1785   *Les 120 Journées de Sodome* (published 1931–37).

1785–1788   Preparation of *Justine* (published 1791) and *Aline et Valcour* (published 1795).

1787   *Les Infortunes de la vertu.*

1787–1788   *Historiettes, Contes et Fabliaux* (published 1926).

1789   2 July, from his cell window, complains to the crowd below of the imminent danger of the Bastille prisoners; he is transferred to Charenton.

1790   Released after almost twelve years of confinement. His wife petitions for separation.

1791   22 October, *Oxtiern* is performed.

1792   3 September, becomes secretary of the Section des Piques. The Sade family's manor at La Coste is pillaged.

1793   December, Sade's name appears erroneously on a list of émigrés. Arrest as a suspected enemy of the Revolution, and confinement in various prisons until 13 October 1794.

1795   *La Philosophie dans le boudoir.*

1797   *La Nouvelle Justine* and *L'Histoire de Juliette.*

1800   *Les Crimes de l'amour.*

1801   6 March, arrested at the office of his publisher, Massé, where police find illustrated editions of *La Nouvelle Justine* and *Juliette.* Imprisoned in Ste.-Pélagie and Bicêtre until 1803, then transferred to Charenton.

1807–1812   Composes *La Marquise de Gange* (published 1813). Produces dramas for the inmates of Charenton.

1810   Death of Mme. de Sade.

1812–1813   *Adelaïde de Brunswick* (published 1954).

1813   *L'Histoire secrète d'Isabelle de Bavière* (published 1953).

1814   2 December, death of the Marquis de Sade at the age of seventy-four.

Chapter One
Life

Early Years and Marriage

The life of the Marquis de Sade has several dominant features: membership in a noble family, though an impoverished one; a series of scandals and debauchery, which led directly or indirectly to imprisonment; and writing as a means of protest against confinement. Sade had the distinction of being a prisoner under the reigns of Louis XV, Louis XVI, the Revolution, and Napoleon. More than twenty-eight of the last forty years of his life were spent in prison. By the age of thirty he had the reputation of a debauchee, and from the days of the Revolution and beyond, he was known as the author of the "infamous" novel *Justine*. More serious charges and epithets would be applied to him by posterity.

Although most of his adult life prior to the long period of confinement was spent at the family estate of La Coste (near Avignon), he was born in Paris on 2 June 1740 at the Hôtel de Condé. Sade's mother, Marie-Eléonore de Maillé de Carman, was related to the house of Condé, and thus the future libertine was designated as a playmate for Louis-Joseph de Bourbon, Prince de Condé. Sade's father was the head of a family which dated back to the twelfth century. He was the Comte de Sade, Seigneur de Saumane et de la Coste, co-seigneur de Mazan, and had a host of other titles. One source of pride in the family's history was the belief that Laure, wife of Hugues de Sade, was espied by Petrarch in 1327 and became his "Laura." The Comte de Sade played an active role in the alliance between France and Spain in 1741, and upon his death in 1767 his distinguished titles and limited resources were passed to his oldest son.[1]

The family name and titles themselves deserve a brief comment. Today the title "Marquis" is inseparable from the Sade name, as if the combined form was a pen name, like Voltaire. A pejorative and disdainful element is also frequently added. On the other hand, we do not automatically associate titles with other writers of noble origins of this period: Montesquieu is identified as just that, without the addition of "Baron." The name also gave rise to special generic terms: sadism, sadistic, sadomasochism, although Sacher-Masoch (the nineteenth-century Austrian writer) was responsible for the creation of at least half of that denomination. Some of the earlier forms of the family name were Sado, de Sadone, de Sazo, and de Sauza (1:3). There were also variations on the author's forename, with serious legal implications for him during the French Revolution. His parents intended him to be baptized Louis-Aldonse-Donatien, but either the servants who relayed the information to the local priest, or the priest himself misunderstood, and he was in fact christened Donatien-Alphonse-François, from whence the commonly used initials D. A. F. In 1792 he signed his name with the more proletarian "Louis" Sade. On 13 December 1792, the name Louis-Alphonse-Donatien Sade appeared on a list of noblemen who were to be executed for having emigrated. Although it was indeed Sade who was intended for execution, and although his name was eventually corrected and removed from the list, he escaped a certain death in 1794 because the officials were ignorant as to which of a succession of prisons actually held him.

The most important blood relative in Sade's life was his uncle, l'abbé de Sade, and after a year spent in the care of his grandmother, the young aristocrat was confided to the abbé in 1745. L'abbé de Sade had obtained the château de Saumane from Sade's father, and spent most of his time there.[2] Saumane is one possible model for the clandestine castles of *Les 120 Journées de Sodome, Justine, La Marquise de Gange,* and others. L'abbé himself may have inspired his young pupil with ideas for the numerous corrupt priests who appear in his work. On the positive side, l'abbé de Sade seems to have done an adequate job with the education of his nephew during the critical formative years. He was also an antiquarian, compiled family records, and wrote a book, *Mémoires pour la vie de Pétrarque* (1764–67), in which he emphasized the legend that Laure de Sade was Petrarch's Laura. He did not appear to pay much attention to his religious vows, however. His lechery was known by Voltaire, who in 1733 scoffed at the uncle's intention of becoming a priest (1:35–36). In 1762, l'abbé de Sade was incarcerated for debauchery with a prostitute (the same charge which was made against his nephew in 1763). He may have attended the bawdy theatrical performances staged by his nephew at La Coste in 1765, with a young

actress, Mlle. de Beauvoisin, posing as the nephew's legitimate wife.
And he may have been amorously involved with Sade's sister-in-
law, Anne-Prospère, herself a "chanoinesse," in 1771 (1:228). Although the uncle was no paragon of virtue, there is no direct proof
that his moral laxity was communicated to his nephew. His harm
was felt in a different way; in 1766, he entered into contact with
Sade's mother-in-law, Mme. de Montreuil, and began spying on
Sade to the point that in May 1775 he requested royal approbation
for the arrest of his nephew as a menace to society and to the family.

At the age of ten, young Sade was removed from his uncle's care
and entered the prestigious collège Louis-le-Grand in Paris. Like
most organized schools of the time, it was staffed by Jesuits and
allowed only male students. Very little information is available
concerning Sade's career as a student, but it is certain that the
program was a rigorous one. One of Sade's instructors at Louis-le-
Grand was significant: l'abbé Jacques-François Amblet, the firm but
intelligent man referred to in the autobiographical passage from
Aline et Valcour, who would remain in contact with Sade and his
turpitudes for many years thereafter. Sade remained in Paris until
1754, when he began military training as a cavalry officer; the Seven
Years' War and the hostilities between France and Prussia afforded
him a brief experience with weaponry and combat. In 1759, he was
promoted to the rank of captain; he was deactivated in 1763.

In the fifth letter of *Aline et Valcour,* the young hero Valcour
narrates his origins and activities to his loved one, in a manner
which closely resembles a portrait of the Marquis de Sade in his
early twenties:

Allied, on my mother's side to the noblest of the kingdom; through my
father, connected with the most distinguished of the province of Langue-
doc; born in Paris in the midst of wealth and abundance, I believed, as
soon as I was able to judge, that nature and good fortune united to shower
me with their gifts; this I believed, because people were stupid enough
to tell me so, and this absurd prejudice made me haughty, tyrannical,
and irascible; it seemed to me that everything should give way to me,
that the whole world should condone my caprices, and that it was up to
me alone to plan and satisfy them. . . .

Born and raised in the palace of the illustrious prince to whom my
mother had the honor of being related and who was about the same age
as me, they endeavored to associate me with him, so that having known
him from childhood, I could call on his support in my future years. . . .

I returned to Paris to pursue my studies under the direction of a firm and intelligent man [Amblet], well suited to the task of educating me, but whom, to my misfortune, I did not keep long enough. War was declared: in a hurry to have me serve, my education was left unfinished, and I left for the regiment at an age when one should naturally have remained in school. . . . The campaigns began, and I can assure you that I performed well. My natural impetuosity, the fiery soul which I had received from nature, merely added strength and energy to that ferocious quality called courage, and which is wrongly considered as the only one necessary to a soldier.[3]

Valcour then enters into a description of his first amorous encounter and seduction, which is very apropos, since the few letters which have survived from this stage in Sade's life express concern from his father regarding Sade's libertine activities, and an occasional expression of remorse from Sade.[4] Because of such activities, the Sade family decided that it was time that their son be properly married. Their choice was Renée-Pélagie de Montreuil (1741–1810), who was to be Sade's greatest personal ally, at least until 1790. Renée-Pélagie was of an enigmatic character. She was not the first choice of her husband, since he had already had at least one affair with a certain Mlle. de Lauris in May 1763, who may have given him venereal disease. Nor was Renée-Pélagie his first choice from among the Montreuil daughters; indeed, Sade preferred the younger Anne-Prospère and eventually ran off with her to Italy. Although his wife bore him three children (Louis-Marie [1767–1809], Donatien-Claude-Armand [1769–1847], and Madeleine-Laure [1771–1844]), she lived in a constant state of turmoil until she insisted on separation in 1790.

Renée-Pélagie was abandoned by her husband four months after their marriage, when Sade escapaded with Jeanne Testard (see below). Testimony from one of the "petites filles" in the 1775 scandal has given rise to the belief that Renée-Pélagie participated in her husband's orgies at home; this is a misinterpretation, based on an isolated remark that she was the "victim" of her husband's frenzied indulgences.[5] She certainly knew of his activities, but her direct involvement in them would have been in total conflict with the probity that she demonstrated elsewhere.

Madame de Sade labored against her own mother's efforts to keep her husband in perpetual confinement. In fact, she attempted to engineer his escape from Miolans in 1773, by dressing as a man and trying to enter the fortress (Sade was eventually successful in plotting his own escape). But such efforts were rewarded with frustration and ingratitude from her spouse. During longer periods of detention, Sade's letters to her contain accusations of infidelity and chastisements for not having seen to his personal whims. Other letters to her are replete with vulgarity.[6] One of the more frequently cited examples of this is the letter dating from the end of 1784, while Sade was in the Bastille. The letter, known as "La Vanille et la Manille," is an encoded script to his wife, with "Manille" referring to masturbation, "arc" used as a reference to his phallus, "flèche" denoting sperm, and so on. Sade complained of his difficulty in releasing his viscous sperm without a partner, and mentioned "horrible episodes" and "violent efforts" as preludes necessary to his orgasm. Of those letters from his wife which have survived, no interest or cooperation on her part is visible.

One other letter by Sade to his wife deserves mention: his "grande lettre" of 20 February 1781. Here, after the exposure of his most notorious scandals, and in the face of perpetual confinement, Sade admitted that he was indeed a libertine, and provided his own defense in grandiose style:

There you have all of my claimed misdeeds, and there are my objections to them which, I swear, I will substantiate by proofs and means whose authenticity will be absolutely impossible to refute. I am therefore guilty of pure and simple libertinism, the likes of which is practised by all men, more or less due to their varying temperament or inclination toward that which they may have received from nature. Everyone has his faults; let us make no comparisons; my tormentors might not profit from such comparisons. (12:276)

Before analyzing the specific acts of which Sade was guilty, one question concerning his wife ought to be aired. After enduring shame and suffering for almost thirty years and after constant efforts to obtain his release, why did she abandon him in 1790, when he was at last freed? One concrete solution was that she, a member of a prestigious family, was in danger of persecution by the Revolutionary tribunals, and was therefore required to leave Paris. Mme. de Sade inevitably felt the despair and fatigue of such long and unrequited efforts, and thus initiated legal proceedings to obtain separation of person and property from her husband. When he was freed, one of Sade's first acts was to accuse his wife of having destroyed the manuscripts which he had confided to her. The plundering of the Bastille prison caused equal if not greater losses of material than those which may have resulted from Renée-Pélagie's censorship.

In addition to the acquisition of a wife in 1763, Sade also obtained a mother-in-law, and his greatest personal enemy. Madame de Montreuil, whom Sade referred to as "the most vile of whores," was initially delighted by the prospect of allying her *petite noblesse de robe* family to the Sade's landed nobility. The Sade clan, on the other hand, was attracted by the possibility of a large dowry. On the eve of the wedding, Mme. de Montreuil referred to Sade as a "most likeable and most desireable son-in-law, by his reasonability, mildness, and good education" (1:88). There is even speculation that she may have been in love with him herself, though this seems rather unlikely.[7] However that may be, the relationship soured. As Sade continued his lechery, Mme. de Montreuil's wrath increased commensurately. She assumed personal responsibility for maintaining the dignity of both family names, and solicited the cooperation of l'abbé de Sade and the family lawyer Gaufridy, as well as officials such as l'inspecteur Marais and powerful *lettres de cachet,* to maintain control over him. With such potent weapons against him, Sade could do little other than attempt literal escape from her authority and prisons. During his stay in Vincennes in February 1777, Sade protested that he had come to Paris to attend the funeral of his mother, only to be arrested by his mother-in-law: "Alas, I asked you in my first letter if it was a second mother or a tyrant that I was to find in you, but you did not leave me in doubt for very long" (1:598). In January of the following year, he wrote to her in his own blood, pleading for his release (1:612). Besides his scandalous behavior, Mme. de Montreuil feared the memoirs which she knew that he was composing, and her fear was appropriate, since Sade's principal means of revenge was by writing. Accordingly, he wrote a "Sort des satellites de la présidente de Montreuil" (Destiny of the henchmen of the *présidente* de Montreuil) in March 1781, with various deaths and disgraces assigned to her relatives and those who cooperated with her (2:82–83). The persecuted and abused mother images in his published works constitute the pursuit of his revenge. Ironically, when Sade could have contributed to the physical arrest of the Montreuil family when he was a revolutionary agent in 1793, he declined to do so.

Affairs

Sade's crimes of passion deserve considerable attention, because these four or five incidents defined his contemporary reputation, incurred the most severe punishments for him, and to an extent, explain posterity's fascination with him.

On 18 October 1763, Jeanne Testard, a fan maker and prostitute, was placed in contact with an anonymous man through a procurer. He took her by carrriage to a "petite maison" near the rue Mouffetard in Paris. They went up to the second floor, and he proceeded to quiz her about her religious beliefs; when she said that she was religious, he responded with blasphemy and told her of his prior sacrileges. He then led her to an adjacent room equipped with a variety of whips, religious images, and indecent pictures. Sade trampled one crucifix, masturbated on another, and told her to trample on it; she hesitated, and he threatened her life.

The night was spent with Sade reading immoral and impious poems to Jeanne Testard. He suggested that she allow him to sodomize her; she apparently refused. He made her promise to meet him the following Sunday, so that they could receive communion together and then defile the hosts. He also made her promise not to reveal what had transpired. When Testard was at last released, she went and informed the police. Sade was arrested nine or ten days later and spent two weeks in Vincennes; he was released on his promise to reform.

Although no other "public" scandals would occur until 1768, Sade was by no means inactive. The surveillance of l'inspecteur Marais reveals affairs with actresses and prostitutes: Mlles. Dorville, Le Claire, Rivière, and Colet. One of the more famous ones was Mlle. de Beauvoisin, to whom Sade gave considerable sums of money. While his wife vacationed in Normandy, Sade took Mlle. de Beauvoisin to La Coste, and together they staged a number of theatrical performances. In Paris, on the other hand, he maintained a series of secret apartments or "petites maisons" to pursue his lusts while in the capital city.

The second major scandal occurred on Easter Sunday (3 April) 1768, and is known as the Rose Keller affair, or "l'Affaire d'Arcueil." Rose Keller, of German origin, was begging in the Place des Victoires. She was approached by Sade himself, who promised her three livres to accompany him. He took her to his country house in Arcueil and, after leaving her alone temporarily, returned and ordered her to disrobe. She protested, and he threatened to kill her and bury her in his garden. He then stripped her himself, forced her onto a couch, and supposedly bound her. Sade disrobed partially, wrapped a kerchief around his head, and whipped her, pausing occasionally to rub a salve or some other ointment in her wounds. After more whipping, he uttered violent yells, having achieved orgasm.

Afterward, Sade freed Keller and allowed her to dress. Left to herself, she made a rope of the bed linens, and scaled down to the rear garden, injuring herself in the final part of the descent. Sade's valet (Langlois) saw her escape and called to her that his master wished to speak with her; she refused and sought refuge among some village women standing nearby.

Maurice Heine has collected most of the official documents and declarations concerning the Keller case.[8] The incident attracted a great deal of attention and contributed to Sade's reputation as "le Marquis de Sade." After Rose Keller's initial testimony to local officials, the case passed to the criminal court at La Tournelle, and then to the Parlement de Paris. The depositions reveal conflicts between the victim's statements, those who interviewed her, and, of course, those of Sade. Rose Keller claimed to have been bound while flogged; there seems to have been no visible sign of binding. She claimed that Sade used a variety of whips and even a knife on her posterior, and that he poured molten wax into her wounds. Examining physicians found little or no evidence of such extremes. In any case, Sade was arrested on 8 April and taken first to Saumur, then to Pierre-Encise (near Lyons), and finally to the Conciergerie, until 16 November. Both the Sade and Montreuil families attempted to quiet the matter, and Keller ultimately accepted 2,400 livres to withdraw her charges. Sade was fined an insignificant sum of money, released by personal order of Louis XV, and ordered to remain at La Coste.

The Keller case received more attention in juridical channels than any of a comparable nature. Gilbert Lely's justification for the notoriety of the affair is that the judge of the Chambre de La Tournelle, le président de Maupeou, was an enemy of Sade's father-in-law, le président de Montreuil, and relished the possibility of dishonoring his rival's family.[9] According to Maurice Heine, the 1768 period bore witness to increasing public outrage at the lack of prosecution of noble families for crimes of the sort; a scapegoat was needed, and the Marquis de Sade lent himself well to such a need.[10]

It was Heine who in 1933 uncovered the documents relating to the case involving the Marseilles prostitutes, the third major scandal in Sade's life. In June of 1772, Sade left La Coste on the pretext of cashing a note for credit. He arrived in Marseilles, accompanied by a valet named Latour, who began a search for young girls for his master. Four girls, ranging in age from eighteen to twenty-three, were assembled in a rented apartment on the morning of 27 June. Sade took a handful of coins from his purse, and the girl who guessed their value was allowed to pass first. Marianne Laverne won, and was taken into a chamber and placed on a bed with Latour, whom Sade addressed as "monsieur le marquis." Sade himself was referred to as Lafleur. He then whipped Marianne and masturbated Latour. Latour was ordered to leave, and Sade encouraged the girl to eat seven or eight candies coated with powder from the cantharis beetle, commonly called Spanish fly.[11] He then asked to sodomize her, and she claimed to have refused. Sade also requested her to flagellate him with a whip barbed with pins; when she lost her courage, he ordered her to leave and purchase a broom.

The second girl was then brought in. Mariette Borelly was beaten with the newly purchased broom, and in turn beat Sade. Meanwhile, Sade recorded the number of blows given and received and carved them on the mantle. Latour returned, and Sade proceeded to sodomize or masturbate him while Latour copulated with Borelly. Similar treatment was experienced by the remaining girls (Rose Coste and Mariannette Laugier): whipping, sodomy with Latour, and so on. Each of the girls was encouraged to eat as many of the candies as possible.

In the evening of that same day, Sade attempted similar orgies with two other women. Those who had participated in the morning's events fell ill (the dosage of cantharide was excessive) and complained to the authorities. They testified in particular concerning Sade's activities with his male servant. Sodomy was at the time punishable by death, but the penalty was rarely, if ever, invoked. A decree was issued for Sade's arrest. In the meantime, he had fled to Italy with his sister-in-law, Anne-Prospère de Launay. The decree charged Sade with attempted poisoning of the Marseilles girls, and Sade and Latour with sodomy. They were burned in effigy in a public square in Aix on 12 September 1772. In December of that year, Sade returned to Chambéry, which was under the jurisdiction of the king of Sardinia. Mme. de Montreuil petitioned for his arrest, and he was confined at Miolans until April of the following year.

While the Marquise de Sade was attempting to buy the silence of the prostitutes involved in the Marseilles case, her mother concentrated her efforts toward the opposite result: permanent riddance of the scourge of her son-in-law. Although she was certainly not delighted over the most recent of Sade's debaucheries, the extent of her wrath is accounted for by the involvement of her other daughter. Anne-Prospère was several years younger than her sister and brother-in-law, had taken preliminary religious vows, and held the title of "chanoinesse," which allowed considerable personal freedom and a modest income. While Sade was fleeing the "prise de corps" order, Anne-Prospère left with him on or about 3 July, and until September they traveled to the major cities in Italy; Sade presented her occasionally as his wife, and, according to one account, enjoyed "all of the intimacies due to this title" (1:279). Anne-Prospère returned to La Coste in early October (she died on 13 May 1781). Whereas her sister's reaction to her escapade with Sade is unknown, Mme. de Montreuil would not tolerate the outrage of incest, and henceforth worked against Sade without respite.

Although Renée-Pélagie was unsuccessful in her attempt to arrange her husband's escape from Miolans in April 1773, Sade engineered his own. With the help of a fellow prisoner, the Baron de l'Allée de Songy, Sade requested that they be allowed to dine in a recently vacated room of the prison. On the night of 30 April, Sade had the valet Latour (imprisoned with him) leave a candle burning in his (Sade's) room. The guards assumed that he was indeed in that room, but eventually became suspicious, and when they opened the room found neither Sade nor the Baron. A kitchen adjacent to the new dining room contained a window which allowed the three to escape through the fortress wall. Sade left behind an ironic letter for his jailor, the Commandant de Launay, in which he thanked him for the kindness and civilities shown during his imprisonment, and expressed the hope that Launay would not suffer as a result of the escape (1:470–72).

In the following months Sade lived more or less openly at La Coste, but was on constant vigil for news of any suspicious arrivals in the neighboring village. Such concern was well founded, since on 6 January 1774 the police raided La Coste on the request of

Mme. de Montreuil. But Sade had received enough prior warning to flee. The "affaire des petites filles" began in December of that year. Sade requested a female procurer, Nanon (Anne Sablonnière), and a male secretary to bring five girls to La Coste, supposedly to hire them as part of the household staff.[12] Subsequent testimony contains allusion to a series of orgies and the possible participation of Renée-Pélagie in them. In any case, three parents complained officially in Lyons of the treatment which their daughters were receiving at La Coste. Mme. de Sade went to Lyons to attempt to quell such complaints. One girl was taken to l'abbé de Sade's castle at Saumane.[13] Another of the girls, Marie Tussin, was placed in the convent of Caderousse, from which she escaped a few months later.

The letters from Mme. de Montreuil to Gaufridy of February–April 1775 contain frequent expressions of concern about the clandestine activities taking place at La Coste. After the five original girls, references are made to the hiring of several others as cooks or scullery maids. One of these, Du Plan, complained of a chamber decorated with bones and skeletons, used as decor for Sade's activities. Eventually the président of the Parlement de Provence complained publicly of Sade's "excès de tout genre" at La Coste. On 11 May 1775, Nanon delivered a child, and Sade was accused of being the father. One week later, l'abbé de Sade called for his nephew's arrest. On 20 June, Nanon fled the chateau and slandered the Sade family. La Marquise de Sade countered with a charge of theft of silver, but only to forestall the scandal provoked by Nanon's outbursts. A *lettre de cachet* was issued, and Nanon was confined in a work house at Arles. But the pressure was sufficiently intense to force Sade to flee again to Italy; he left on 26 July 1775, and did not (dare) return till the summer of the following year. During his exile, one of his missives to Gaufridy contains a humorous reference to the scope of his reputation at this point: "I can hear you say: Sir, new misdeeds have prolonged your misfortunes.—But hear also my reply to that: Sir, it is precisely my misfortunes, my discredit, my current position which prolong my sufferings, and as long as I am not vindicated, not one cat will be beaten in the province without people saying: *it was the Marquis de Sade*" (1:566).

There would be a sequel to this fourth scandal with the girls at La Coste, before the twelve years of uninterrupted confinement which began in 1778. Near the end of October 1776, Catherine Trillet was hired as a cook. At this time money was in extremely short supply at the residence, because Sade's seigneurial income had been impounded as a result of the Marseilles affair. Mme. de Montreuil sent just enough money for the household's needs for the winter. Catherine's father had heard of the licentious events taking place at La Coste and requested that his daughter be released.

Having received no satisfaction, Trillet appeared at La Coste at midday on 17 January; he insisted that his daughter (called "Justine" by her master) be freed. Sade attempted to usher him to the door. Trillet drew a pistol and fired at Sade at point blank range, but the gun misfired. Trillet ran to the nearby village of La Coste and there slandered Sade. Catherine summoned her father back to the chateau and tried to calm him; he returned in the evening and fired another shot in the courtyard, where he thought that he had seen the lord of the castle. He then withdrew to an inn.

Sade endeavored to bring charges against Trillet; such an effort was difficult, since he was in constant danger of arrest himself. Having learned that his mother was near death, Sade set out for Paris, as did Renée-Pélagie, accompanied by Catherine, who refused to return to her father in spite of his insistence. Sade arrived in Paris on 8 February, learned that his mother had died on 14 January, and on 13 February he was arrested by Marais, the same officer who had taken him to Pierre-Encise nine years earlier. The arrest was authorized by a *lettre de cachet* obtained by Mme. de Montreuil.

No direct proof of debauchery involving Sade and Catherine Trillet has been revealed. Her father was acting largely on hearsay evidence and gossip. Nor was Catherine Trillet a likely model for Sade's *Justine.* She simply was not present long enough to have inspired the sinister episodes of Sade's classic. But other aspects of the Trillet case, such as being fired on in his own chateau, are elements worthy of any gothic thriller.

These scandals are crucial to an understanding of Sade; they show what he was capable of, what his desires were, and the limits of his actions. The Testard case of 1763 indicates a flair for blasphemy and sodomy. Fascination with algolognia (the desire to be whipped) and sacrilege surfaced in the episode with Rose Keller (since he offered to hear her confession). In both the Marseilles case and that of the young girls at La Coste, Sade revealed his predilection for the exotic (use of aphrodisiacs which, ironically, were not very stimulating, since the women became ill from them), for large numbers of participants in his escapades, and the tendency toward bisexuality. His own view of the scandals was provided at the end of his "grande lettre" to Mme. de Sade: "Yes, I am a libertine, I confess; I have thought of everything imaginable in that vein, but I certainly did not practice all that I thought of, nor would I ever do so. I am a libertine, but I am not a criminal nor a murderer . . ." (12:276). Given the evolution of morals and attitudes from Sade's age to modern times, he was indeed guilty of aberration and cruelty, but not to the extent of meriting the death sentence issued in 1772. In his personal actions there were violence and threats of death, but the murders and tortures that cloud the more extreme of his literary creations (*Les 120 Journées de Sodome* and *Juliette*) were not acted out by the writer; such horrors were obviously impossible for one man to commit.

The specific charge of "débauche outrée" leveled against him as a result of his encounter with Jeanne Testard is noteworthy. The term itself could apply to misdemeanors or to the most savage carnal indulgence. It can be compared to the statutes governing conspiracy in the United States today—laws which can be applied to an extremely wide range of misconduct, or merely to planning. The same ambiguity exists concerning immoral publications. If one looked among French laws for statutes relating to pornography, a great deal of material would not be found. Although the *Code civil* underwent significant revision from the monarchy, through the Declaration of the Rights of Man, to the definitive form of 1810 (all of which affected Sade), and although he was arrested at his publisher's in 1801, where the police seized copies of *Juliette* and *la Nouvelle Justine,* less attention was paid to the content of these works than to their attempted sale and to the reputation of their author. The same is true today in France. The section of the *Code civil* relating to what we might consider pornography is entitled "Outrage aux bonnes moeurs." That which constitutes obscenity or "outrage" is imprecise and vaguely defined. Elements of Sade's works are worthy of being burned, but not necessarily their author. The outrage experienced by the Montreuil family as a result of the son-in-law's deviations was the more direct cause for his persecution.

Imprisonment, Revolution, and Writing

When Sade was arrested in Paris by Marais on 13 February 1777, a period of almost twelve years of uninterrupted confinement began.

In a plaintive letter to his wife shortly thereafter, he demonstrated that his adaptation to imprisonment was no better than in previous instances: "I feel that it is absolutely impossible for me to endure such a cruel condition any longer. My blood is too warm to bear such terrible harm. I want to turn the effects of my wrath against myself, and if I am not out in four days, nothing is more certain than I will smash my head against the walls" (1:597). One glimpse of hope for freedom appeared in the following year (1778), when Sade was taken from Vincennes to Aix-en-Provence, for a review of the judgment issued in 1772. The court judged him guilty of debauchery in the Marseilles incident and fined him fifty livres, but instead of being released Marais informed Sade that the *lettre de cachet* granted in February 1777 was still in effect and that he was to be taken back to Vincennes. In the evening of 16 July at an inn near Valence, Sade managed to overcome one of his guards, knock down another one, and flee. While Marais and his men conducted an intensive search, Sade hired two peasants to guide him to the banks of the Rhone, and he eventually made his way back to La Coste.

Sade was able to enjoy thirty-nine days of freedom there, and when Marais did finally catch up with him on 26 August, he vented his frustration on his escaped prisoner and promised that he would be locked up for the rest of his days. The estate at La Coste had been virtually abandoned, with the exception of a woman named Gothon, the mistress of Sade's valet La Jeunesse, and Mlle. de Rousset, a housekeeper to whom Sade frequently wrote after his arrest, and who would assist Madame de Sade in her efforts to obtain Sade's release. It was with these two women that Sade spent his brief period of escape.

The return to Vincennes for four and one-half years concretized the cycle of libertinism-prison-writing in Sade's life, the writing serving as an escape from physical detention.[14] With few exceptions, the prisoner was permitted to have pen and paper in order to write; Renée-Pélagie was allowed periodic visits, and supplied books, clothing, and specially prepared culinary items. Near the end of 1783, he described himself to her in three short lines as "haughty, angry, touchy, extreme in everything, due to a disordered imagination about morals which has never had its equal, in short, there you have me; and one more thing: either kill me or take me as I am, because I will not change." In the following years, he would complain, understandably, of the hardships and illness contracted while in prison, and in particular of problems related to his eyes, an affliction which surely resulted from reading too much. One further incident from the period of incarceration in Vincennes is of note: on 28 June 1780 the captain of the guard at Vincennes reported that Sade, after having been denied his usual walk in the courtyard for insulting the staff, espied Mirabeau being allowed that privilege, and insulted him with a number of vulgarities. Although Sade knew who Mirabeau was, he challenged him to reveal his name, and threatened to cut off Mirabeau's ears if he were ever released. Mirabeau, who was a distant cousin of Sade, replied: "My name is that of a man of honor who has never dissected nor poisoned women" (2:70). Mirabeau was released in that same year and died in 1791, before his royalist sympathies would have brought certain execution.

In calmer moments, Sade spent his time reading and laying the plans for his thoughts and literary works. In his own words, the ideas of La Mettrie and D'Holbach had the greatest impact on his own philosophy; his indebtedness to them will be discussed in the following chapter. He also avidly read Montaigne, Voltaire, Rousseau, historical works, and travel literature; when he was transferred to the Bastille in 1784, the inventory of his possessions there included books by Fielding, Marmontel, Fénelon, Marivaux, the *Iliad,* Chasles, and other works of fiction (2:163–66). In the Bastille, he pursued his taste for history, novels, poetry, and drama; a list of his holdings as of 1787 contains, among other items, works by Hume, Ninon de Lenclos, l'abbé Dubos, Cervantes, Mme. Riccoboni, Fanny Burney, and even a copy of Laclos's *Liaisons dangereuses.* It suffices to say that Sade was familiar with the major philosophical and literary productions of his time; more will be said on their impact in subsequent paragraphs.

The 1785–88 period produced some of Sade's most significant writings: *Les 120 Journées de Sodome, Justine, Aline et Valcour,* and a group of shorter works, *Historiettes, Contes et Fabliaux.* Imprisonment had become a reality, and with the prospect of release becoming more remote, Sade turned to writing as a substitute for actual freedom. From simple imitation to the most violent of writings, he wrote feverishly, submitting a few of his manuscripts to the conservative scrutiny of Madame de Sade, and stashing others in the recesses of his cell wall. *Les 120 Journées de Sodome* was written on a roll of paper thirteen yards long, so that it could be easily concealed from search. Sade worked quickly, using only rough sketches of his characters and a skeletal outline, and was capable of writing 4,000 words on a productive day. [15] When circumstances permitted, he revised and edited, making notes to himself in the second person formal (the "vous"). Sade was also fascinated with mathematical and encoded formulas; they served as a means of frank communication with his wife, and allowed him to bypass prison inspection and censorship; they also reveal his anguish as a prisoner. One of the more ill-disguised examples was cited above: the "Vanille et la manille" letter, where he complained of his difficulty in achieving orgasm. Anything which might contain a coincidental relationship with past dates of significance or numerical consistency was of special interest, as seen in the following letter to his wife:

Today, Thursday 14 December 1780, the 1,400th day, the 200th week and the arrival of the 46th month that we have been separated, having received from you sixty-eight bi-weekly packages and one hundred letters, and this one from me being the 114th. These last three items relate only to the second period of detention. As for the first three, it will forever be one and the same, since my real misfortune begins only on that day which separated us, and since I have never counted nor never will count anything except from this period. (12:254)

Sade's *Journal inédit* from the years 1807–14 is filled with similar frustrated attempts at guessing the date of his eventual liberation.

Sade's release would be wrought by a blanket amnesty granted to all prisoners of the *ancien régime* in 1790. While awaiting that edict, he could do little less than to complain and pursue his work. Another prisoner-writer, Madame Roland, who was awaiting death in 1793, observed: "It is to live a second time to retrace the steps of one's career; and what better is there to do in prison than to transport elsewhere one's existence through a happy story or by interesting memories?" [16] When Sade was freed during the decade of the Revolution, his life became anticlimactic compared to the excesses and comfort of previous years, but he had already acquired experiences and memories sufficient to populate an entire fantastic world.

On 2 July 1789, Sade indulged in a bit of rabble-rousing. Improvising a megaphone from a rain spout, he yelled to the crowd assembled below that the throats of the Bastille's prisoners were being slashed, and that they must be liberated. As a consequence, and because of the volatility of the moment, he was transferred two days later to the convent at Charenton, which housed primarily the insane. On 14 July, the Bastille was stormed and razed. Sade claimed to have lost fifteen volumes of manuscript works in that raid, and bitterly reproached his wife for not having done more to retrieve them. On 13 March 1790, the National Assembly abolished the authority of all *lettres de cachet* and on 12 April, Sade left Charenton: "I am free at last," he wrote, "but penniless; I fell into the midst of Paris with one *louis* in my pocket, not knowing where to go, eat or sleep" (12:467). Totally abandoned by family and by his wife (by this time Renée-Pélagie had been granted her separation request), Sade filled the void with Marie-Constance Quesnet, and moved in with her on 1 November 1790. Marie-Constance was much younger than Sade; she had done some acting, and when her husband left her, she remained with Sade almost uninterruptedly until his death in 1814. He referred to her by the name "Sensible" and dedicated a new edition of *Justine* to her in 1795. He was also very generous to her in his last will and testament.

By virtue of residential location, Sade was assigned membership in the Section des Piques in Paris; he eventually became the secretary of that unit in 1792. His duties included participation in the inspection and administration of public hospitals, and in April 1793, he was nominated as a juror with magisterial powers in cases involving forged *assignats* (promissory notes). His father-in-law, the président de Montreuil, appeared before his tribunal, and Sade observed with some delight to Gaufridy: "I want to inform you of two things which will surprise you. The président de Montreuil came to see me. And you must guess the other one! . . . I will give you a hundred tries . . . I am a judge, yes, a judge! . . . an arraignment judge! Who would have thought of that, my dear lawyer, who would ever have thought of that! You can see that my head is whitening and that I am beginning to be wise . . ." (2:367). His recently acquired power was not abused, however, and he could not force himself to further complicate the existence of the already endangered Montreuil family.

In the face of the chaos and economic instability of this darkest period of the French Revolution, Sade was compelled to write in order to subsist, and he concentrated his efforts on the theater. Although *Oxtiern* was the only one of Sade's plays to have been fully performed (by the Théâtre Molière in 1791), he continued to circulate the manuscripts of his dramatic works as late as 1813.

One of the greatest mysteries of Sade's life was that he was able to survive the French Revolution at all. His reputation of infamy had been established as early as 1772, and his aberrations and erotic works were not forgotten. Whereas most people of noble origin were forced to emigrate, if they were indeed able to do so, Sade's presence in Paris during the Reign of Terror was audacious and ill-advised. To his chagrin, the château of La Coste was pillaged and eventually destroyed in September 1792, and the furnishings were carried off to the nearby commune. Sade's increasing alarm was justified since, in spite of his cooperation with Revolutionary activities, he was again arrested on 8 December 1793. The name of Louis-Alphonse-Donatien Sade had appeared on a list of nobles scheduled for prosecution in the preceding year, and in addition to that accusation Sade was cited for having used Greek and Roman historical precedents as evidence of the impossibility of establishing a republican government in France. His incarceration may have saved his life, because in the rapid succession of incumbent regimes between 1793 and 1794 administrative affairs were very confused. Sade was first confined to the Madelonettes prison. He petitioned his old allies in the Section des Piques to intervene on his behalf, but to no avail for the time being. In 1794, he was transferred first to Les Carmes, then Saint-Lazare, and finally to the Picpus asylum. During the review of his case, confusion reigned as to his true name and identity, and in July 1794, when twenty-eight enemies of the republic were condemned to death, "Aldonze" Sade was declared "absent" and thus spared. From the window of his chamber in Picpus, which he ironically called a "terrestrial paradise," Sade could appreciate the gravity of the situation:

All of a sudden the site for executions was placed squarely underneath our windows, and the cemetery for the guillotined in the very middle of our yard. We have buried 1,800 of them in thirty-five days, one third of which came from our ill-fated institution. . . . My official detention, the guillotine under my eyes, have done one hundred times more harm to me than all of the Bastilles imaginable. (2:419–20)

Finally, on the strength of endorsement from his revolutionary section and sheer luck, he was set free on 13 October 1794. But Sade's last major period of freedom was not a pleasant one. He was plagued with money problems and had difficulty obtaining royalties from his published works (*Aline et Valcour*, *La Nouvelle Justine*, and *Juliette*), and had even less success in obtaining revenues from his estates in Provence. His health was deteriorating also, as can be felt in a letter to Gaufridy of 24 June 1796: "Money, money, send me money, or I will beg the doctors to do me in . . ." (2:433). Instead of writing more dramas and experiencing the satisfaction of seeing them performed, Sade worked as a custodian at the theater of Versailles in 1799.

Although Sade's name was definitively removed from the list of émigrés in 1798, his legal troubles were not finished. On 6 March 1801, he was arrested at the house of his publisher Massé, where police seized diverse copies of *La Nouvelle Justine* and *Juliette*. A similar raid was conducted at St.-Ouen, where Sade and Mme. Quesnet had been living, and where there was purported to be a secret chamber decorated with tapestries "representing the most obscene subjects, taken for the most part from the infamous novel *Justine*."[17] Sade claimed to be merely a copyist of the editions which bore his autograph notes, but he was nonetheless taken off to Sainte-Pélagie until 1803, then transferred for a brief period to Bicêtre, and afterward to Charenton, for the remainder of his life. The usual appeals and protests of innocence brought no more relief from the Bonaparte administration than from previous ones. After one such appeal in 1804 to Fouché (minister of police), a report was issued designating the prisoner as "an incorrigible man in a perpetual state of libertine insanity," and "of a character opposed to any and all cooperation" (2:549–50). The decision was made to leave him in Charenton at the expense of his family, and for the sake of its honor. Sade did maintain occasional contact with this family that agreed to keep him locked away. He expressed opposition to the marriage of his son Donatien in 1808; his oldest son, Louis-Marie, was killed in Napoleon's service in 1809.

Literary activity again became the means by which Sade countered the ignominy and pernicious effects of being surrounded with the insane. Accordingly, in 1803–4, he undertook a reorganization of his works written prior to that date.[18] Ironically, the talents of this "infamous" author were put to use in the insane asylum. The directorship of Charenton felt that it would be therapeutic for the inmates to attend theatrical performances. Such optimism was not unanimous: in 1808, a visiting inspector at Charenton complained of the contact between patients and the "infamous author of *Justine*"

(2:557). In 1812, H. de Colins, a former cavalry officer on tour of public institutions, voiced a similar complaint:

The first thing which presented itself to my eyes was his [the asylum director's] intimate connection with a monster [*Desade* written in the margin] condemned to public execration and whom the government believed to have sentenced to a perpetual detention, in order that society be rid of him. It is apparent that I will here speak of the author of the infamous novel *Justine;* for to him alone can such a qualification apply. . . . What faith can be inspired by a director who allows access and favor by a creature to whom I cannot give the name of man; a director who consents to take in such a panegyrist, who gives a public performance of his own play and for his own aggrandizement; a fitting Horace for such a Maecenas.[19]

Elsewhere in his lengthy report, Colins observed other practices in the asylum which displeased him: the mistreatment of prisoners, which included a "bain de surprise" (sudden immersion in cold water), the filth of the accommodations, the lack of proper waste disposal, etc. If Sade was not mad when he entered Charenton, he assuredly suffered mental deterioration from such deplorable conditions, and Peter Weiss must have had Colins's description of Charenton in mind when he composed *Marat-Sade.*

No authentic portrait of Sade has survived,[20] but we have seen verbal images of him at various intervals, from his correspondence and the observations. In the final months of his life, he appeared as a broken man, suffering from gout, rheumatism, and eye disease.[21] At the rather advanced age of seventy-four, he was reported to be sexually active; Madame Quesnet was allowed to visit him regularly, as was the adolescent daughter of another friend, Madeleine Leclerc.

In the chapters which follow some attention has been paid to the chronological order in which Sade's works were written. But a structural-thematic approach is more practical. *Justine* is grouped with *Juliette,* since the two works have much in common but were written a number of years apart; *Justine* and *Les 120 Journées de Sodome* are near contemporaries but are quite different, and thus it is more fitting that the latter be treated with the rest of Sade's philosophical tracts, although philosophy can be found in everything he wrote. Special consideration will be given to *Aline et Valcour,* since it typifies the forms and ideas used by other writers of the period. The most homogeneous of Sade's fictional creations are his last three historical novels: *La Marquise de Gange, Adelaïde de Brunswick,* and *Isabelle de Bavière;* they pursue the theme of persecution of virtue and mistreatment of women begun in *Justine,* but are vastly more subdued than the earlier works. Sade is not the most pleasant author to read. In some instances, he is brutal and repulsive. With that caution given, we should also observe that considerable attention will be paid to the summaries of Sade's works; this appears to be necessary, since the author of *Justine* and *Juliette* was indeed guilty of some of the charges leveled against him, but at other times is innocuous and even innocent.

Chapter Two
Philosophical Discourses
Early Works and Sources

The dozen years of uninterrupted confinement from 1778 to 1790 allowed Sade to read extensively and formulate the nucleus of his system of thought. This task was completed midway through the 1780 decade. To a point, Sade conforms to the main patterns of thought of the Age of Enlightenment, but he transcends the more prudent limits established by earlier eighteenth-century writers.

Sade's first known work is a short discourse (twelve pages in the Tête de Feuilles edition) entitled *Dialogue entre un prêtre et un moribond;* it was written while Sade was in the Vincennes prison, and was published in 1926 by Maurice Heine. It would be difficult to find a better introduction to Sade's revolt against convention or to his blunt hedonism. What one would normally expect from an interview between a priest and a dying man (confession, submission, absolution) is transformed into a powerful exposition of the moribund's atheism, followed by the destruction of the validity of theology and the degradation of the interviewer. To the first question concerning repentance, the dying man replies that he regrets only not having understood during his lifetime the full force of nature and the strength of his desires. The priest counters with the idea of a good God, only to be told that nature is the corrupt product of the traditional God, and a vile trap for its creatures. The dying man cannot believe in God, because God is a phenomenon which he can neither feel nor touch; he challenges the priest to define or describe God, or concede the point. The dialectic pursues as follows:

> *Priest:* And who can regulate everything as it is, if not an omnipotent and omniscient hand?
>
> *Dying man:* Must it not be that gunpowder ignites when fire is applied to it?
>
> *Priest:* Yes.

Dying man:	And what wisdom do you find in that?
Priest:	None.
Dying man:	It is then possible that certain things are necessary with wisdom, and it is consequently possible that everything derives from a primary cause, with neither reason or wisdom behind this primary cause.
Priest:	What is your point?
Dying man:	To prove to you that everything can be what it is and as you see it, without a wise or rational cause behind it, and that natural effects must have natural causes, with no need for unnatural ones, such as your god. . . . Thus, at the point when your god becomes good for nothing, he is perfectly useless. . . . (14:58)

The dying man totally dominates the remainder of the dialogue, rejecting miracles and the idea of martyrs, and insisting that Jesus Christ is no better than Muhammed, Moses, or Confucius. All that exists in nature must exist and must be good, including vice and virtue, which balance one another (14:63). The dying man adds one more point: the entirety of human morality is included in this message: render others as happy as one wishes to be oneself (14:64). Faced with these radical arguments, the inept priest can do no more than to call for the heavens to open and for God to pour down thunder and lightning. In the abrupt conclusion, the vigorous dying man announces that he has nearby six beautiful women to cavort with as his last act on earth, and invites the priest to partake of their charms. The priest accepts.

Dialogue, like the novel and *conte philosophique,* was a common means used for the exposition and justification of ideas in eighteenth-century France. Through the verbal exchange in dialogue, the weakness of an erroneous thesis was brought out, and the merits of a more convincing rationale were underscored. Voltaire used dialogue extensively in his articles in *Le Dictionnaire philosophique* and throughout his *contes.* Rousseau's confession of deism, known as the "Profession de foi du vicaire savoyard" (*Emile,* part 4), contributed as much to the condemnation and burning of *Emile* as the educational elements therein; it also used the dialectical form. Diderot utilized dialogue abundantly; the larger portion of *Jacques le fataliste* and the discussion of the words written in the big book "là-haut" are interchanges between Jacques and his master, as are *Le Neveu de Ra-*

meau, the *Entretien entre Diderot et D'Alembert,* parts of the *Supplément au voyage de Bougainville,* and so on. Sade of course knew of these major thinkers of the century; he possessed the complete works of Voltaire and Rousseau, and made an occasional reference to Diderot. (His infrequent use of the latter is explained by the fact that most of Diderot's principal works were published posthumously.) The impact of these writers on Sade will be discussed in greater detail in the chapters which follow.

Two other short works of the same period and of similar content deserve attention. The first is Sade's *Pensée* (14:67–70). Its opening statement parallels the argument of the *moribond:* "God is absolutely to man the same as colors are to a person who is born blind; it is impossible to imagine them." Since a supreme being can be described only in tangential fashion, he cannot exist:

In regard to this grand mystery which is qualified by the name of God, we are this society of blind men; we have invented a thing which we believed necessary, but which has no other existence than the need which we once had for creating it. . . . Man said: "One thing will be called virtue because it harms me." Such are the hopeless rules of the society of blind men whose laws have no intrinsic reality. (14:68).

It is curious that Sade did not know of Diderot's *Lettre sur les aveugles,* written in 1749, which entailed the author's imprisonment, also in Vincennes. According to Diderot's *Lettre,* since blind people cannot see and appreciate the beauty of God's creation, the creation does not necessarily exist. In the final paragraph of his *Pensée,* Sade attacks the ontological argument for the existence of a divinity, that is, the Cartesian formula "Je pense, donc je suis," and since we have a notion of perfection, that perfection (God, according to Descartes) must exist. For Sade, this rationale is as invalid as the proof of God's existence by the beauty and harmony of the universe from the perspective of the blind.

Apart from his dramas, Sade completed only one work in verse. He used a four-page poem, *La Vérité* (written in 1787, published in 1961) to reiterate his hostility against theism and virtue. The two fundamental points of the *Dialogue entre un prêtre et un moribond* and his *Pensée* are magnified poetically:

> Yes, vain illusion, my soul detests you,

And I protest that, in order to further convince you,
I wish that for a moment you could exist,
To have the pleasure to better insult you. . . .

Nothing is forbidden by his murderous laws
And incest, rape, robbery, parricide,
The pleasures of Sodom and delights of Sapho,
All that which harms man or entombs him is,
We can be sure, but a means of pleasing him.

(14:81–84)

In the margin of his poem, Sade wrote down an idea for a frontis-piece; it was to depict a nude man sodomizing and stabbing a woman at the same time, with the three elements of the Trinity and other religious images at their feet (14:88). Verbal images in the lines not quoted from the poem are similar to the planned illustration in their defamation.

Violent atheism, defilement of all that is sacred, and hatred of the divine are the tenets of these three early works. The subtitle of *La Vérité* is noteworthy: "document found among the papers of La Mettrie." It indicates a specific source of inspiration for Sade's radical thought. Julien de La Mettrie (1709–51) used the materialist ideas of early Greek writers to compose his *L'homme machine* in 1747. Having also worked with anatomy and physiology, he concluded that man's soul is that which thinks in him, and is not necessarily a spiritual gift. Man's body is a machine, but so complex that we can never understand it. The dominant faculty, imagination, is subject to violent passions, resulting in a vicious, animalistic nature. If man is indeed mechanical, then the notions of remorse or deviation from virtue need not be our concern. La Mettrie did not resort to the extreme of atheism; he excluded the question of God's existence as being unverifiable.[1] But his work was sufficiently bold to force him to flee his native Netherlands and seek refuge at the court of Frederick the Great, who gave him a pension.

Obviously, Sade venerated the great names of French Enlight-enment thought. His admiration of Rousseau bordered on hero worship.[2] But for his direct ideological borrowings, he turned to other *philosophes,* particularly D'Holbach. Paul Heinrich (Baron D') Holbach (1723–89) is best known for his *Système de la nature* (1770) and *Le Christianisme dévoilé* (1761). He contributed more than 400 articles to *l'Encyclopédie*. D'Holbach's definition of atheists in *Système de la nature* is analogous to the one provided by Sade's dying man:

What is an atheist? It is a man who destroys myths which are harmful to his species, in order to lead men back to nature, experience, and reason. It is a thinker who, having contemplated matter and its energy, its properties and behavior, does not need to invent fictitious powers, imaginary deities, and the like, in order to explain the phenomena of the universe and the operations of nature.[3]

Like Sade, D'Holbach wondered how men could be expected to worship an idea (God) which they could not comprehend. He attacked miracles, orthodox religion, and Christ in particular, as being hoaxes.[4] Instead of traditional belief and conformity to general behavior, D'Holbach substituted the golden rule of beneficence: "Faites du bien." Sade was so captivated by D'Holbach's *Système de la nature* that he asked his wife to send him a copy of it, so that he could compare it to Bergier's refutation of it (2:143). D'Holbach was also cited in *Juliette* (8:30).

The ideas of La Mettrie and D'Holbach are at the heart of Sade's thought in the 1790 decade, and, as will be seen, those of Voltaire, Rabelais, and others would also be used. The notion and practice of beneficence would gradually disappear, but Sade's aversion to religion was firmly implanted. When compared to the attacks against men, women, God, and religion in *La Nouvelle Justine, Juliette,* and *Les 120 Journées de Sodome,* Sade's *Dialogue entre un prêtre et un moribond* and *Pensée* are, in fact, mild.

La Philosophie dans le boudoir

Similar to the preceding short treatises, *La Philosophie dans le boudoir* is a set of seven dialogues. It is a good introduction to the most scandalous works of the Marquis de Sade. It is a special blend of fiction and philosophy to which Sade must have given considerable time and effort. *La Philosophie dans le boudoir* could be considered as the author's "purest" creation, were it not for the abundance of scatology in it. From that point of view, it is an intermediary work, expounding on the ideas outlined briefly in the *Dialogue entre un prêtre et un moribond,* and setting the stage for the amplification of carnal passions in *Les 120 Journées de Sodome.*

La *Philosophie dans le boudoir* (published in 1795) has as its subtitle "Les Instituteurs immoraux." This is precisely the role of Madame de Saint-Ange who explains to her brother, the Chevalier de Mirvil: "I am an amphibious creature; I like everything, I enjoy anything, I want to combine all of the variations" (3:371). Her project is the initiation into libertinism of a beautiful fifteen-year-old girl, Eugénie de Mistival, whom she espied in a convent and whose father is a frequent companion in perversion. To aid in this lesson in immorality, Madame de Saint-Ange engages the help of the notorious Dolmancé, a thirty-two-year-old rake who specializes in sodomy. The lesson begins in the third dialogue, in Saint-Ange's boudoir. Since the young Eugénie has just left her convent school, her instructor begins with all of the anatomical features of the male and female bodies, explained in both quasi-biological and vulgar terms. Eugénie is approached frontally by Mme. de Saint-Ange, and dorsally by Dolmancé, and experiences her first orgasm. Practice is then followed by Dolmancé's abstractions on the words virtue and religion, words which Eugénie must henceforth eliminate from her vocabulary, as well as any other ideas of religious devotion. A rapid shift back to multiple sex scenes is concluded by more of Dolmancé's expositions. If several lines could convey the essence of the degradation process in the work, they would be these: "Fuck, in a word, fuck; it is for this that you were brought into the world; no other limit to your pleasures than those of your strength and will, no place, time, or person excluded; at any time, or place, all men should serve your revelries" (3:404). Eugénie learns quickly; in a few hours she equals and surpasses the intense lust of her tutors. To increase the potential sexual variations of the group, a crude and enormously endowed gardener named Augustin is ushered into the chamber of Mme. de Saint-Ange, as is her brother, who copulates with her and the others. Eugénie passes from the role of victim to aggressor: when asked by the rakes which person she holds in greatest contempt, she names her mother. As might be expected, Mme. de Mistival bursts in to protest, and is stripped and raped by her daughter, then by the others. Eugénie could not be more candid: "Here I am incestous, adulterous, a sodomite, and all that for a girl who was deflowered only today! What progress, my friends!" (3:542). To complete the humiliation of the mother, Mme. de Mistival is assaulted by Dolmancé's syphilitic valet, Lapierre. Eugénie's animosity toward her mother culminates with the sewing of both her lower orifices, so that the disease implanted in her will remain. The gruesome attack is followed by a banquet.

A few of the "finer" details of *Philosophie dans le boudoir* recall experiences in Sade's career as a libertine. The danger posed by syphilis may be a reminiscence of Sade's first love affair with Mlle. de Lauris. Of further note is the introduction of valets and ignorant domestics in orgiastic scenes, as happened in Marseilles and at La Coste. The victimization of Eugénie may be viewed as the execution in fiction of Sade's libidinous aims and desires regarding his wife and/or sister-in-law. Above all, the maternal roles in Sadian fiction are abused: Mme. de Bressac *(Justine)*, Mme. de Blamont *(Aline et Valcour)*, and Mme. de Franval *(Eugénie de Franval)*, but not to the extent witnessed here. The prison of Vincennes and the Bastille gave Sade twelve years to distill and refine his means of retribution for the woman who kept him there.

La Philosophie dans le boudoir is erotic and imaginative but tends toward repetition. Its structure alternates layers of pornography and digression, each repeated six times or so. As in *Juliette* and to a lesser extent *Justine,* Sade interrupts his fictional cadre so many times that he becomes monotonous. One redeeming feature of the fictional approach is the presence of theatrics. Calling to mind Sade's endeavors at directing plays at La Coste and (later) at Charenton, we find scene indications at the beginning of each of the seven dialogues, and stage directions throughout them. Lists of characters in each scene are also provided. The author orchestrates the various sex combinations, but is aware, at the same time, that his repetitions may bore the reader, as witnessed in the following "aside": "Augustin, Dolmancé and the Chevalier act in unison; the fear of being monotonous prevents us from giving their expressions which, in such cases, are completely identical" (3:456). When a particular character is not involved in an acrobatic scene, he or she is expected to observe and encourage the others. Sade's own experiences with group sex involved multiple actors; with the addition of theatrical directions, he invites the reading audience to view and participate also.[5]

Dolmancé is Sade's spokesman. He provides the philosophy of *Philosophie dans le boudoir.* In conformity to his Sadian ancestors who were steeped in the ideas of La Mettrie, he eliminates from Eugénie's curriculum all notions of virtue, religion, and their accouterments. While people outside are dying of hunger and the executioner's blade, he is safely within, at liberty to indulge in his lascivious practices. Dolmancé is an atheist for the same basic reasons expressed by Sade's *moribond:* creation cannot equal the creator, just as a watch cannot be the clockmaker. Therefore God and nature must be different (3:394). In place of those outdated notions he offers abortion in order to preserve sexual freedom, flagellation and other forms of cruelty, and incest as practiced by Mme. de Saint-Ange and her brother. His trinity is composed of sodomy, sacrilege, and cruelty (3:431). His most important lesson to Eugénie is: "turn your entire imagination to the most extreme deviations of libertinism; consider that you are going to see the most beautiful mysteries unfold before your eyes; crush any inhibitions under your feet; prudishness never was a virtue" (4:444). The pupil is impatient to oblige. The lesson has succeeded, and we are left to imagine that the number of victims of the newly ordained pervert will equal those of her teachers. Some modern interpreters might feel that Eugénie is freed from her conformist past, or that she is emancipated by Dolmancé. There is a process of *déniaisement* involved in *La Philosophie dans le boudoir;* Vera Lee makes the important point that Sade pushes this process to its logical extreme.[6] But as opposed to the normal result of a *bildungsroman,* where progress is made, where information is acquired and the naive are demystified, Sade removes the outer veils and external barriers from Eugénie's past, but then continues so far in his deification of lust that lust becomes another restriction.

The longest of all of Dolmancé's digressions is found in the fifth dialogue. It constitutes nearly one third of *La Philosophie dans le boudoir* and is entitled "Français, encore un effort si vous voulez être républicains."[7] Assuming that *La Philosophie* was written in 1792–93, it must be said that this political pamphlet (supposedly purchased in the street by Dolmancé before entering Saint-Ange's chambers), is the expression of Sade's views of the French Revolution.[8] But Sade's treatise has little to do with actual revolutionary events. Dolmancé's reading merely reiterates his atheistic and naturalistic ideas expressed elsewhere. One point stands out, however: the alliance of the *scepter* and the *censer* (the Bourbon monarchy and the Catholic church) must be eliminated. Sade's spokesman is opposed to the capital execution of criminals, perhaps a reflection of the death sentence of 1772. In contrast, Dolmancé argues in favor of occasional murder, with the absurd rationale that no harm is performed against society in such selective cases, and that the practice has allowed the revolution to be permanently established. The political soapbox permits him to justify his special predilection (sodomy), followed by a pseudohistorical account of its origin. "Français, encore un effort . . . " is politically the same act of defiance as the violence committed against the person of Mme. de Mistival. It is the written form of citizen Sade's claimed act of throwing an irate letter into the carriage of King Louis XVI as the latter was forced back from Varennes to Paris (2:310–11). It cost the ex-marquis, now living in revolutionary Paris as Louis Sade, nothing to pursue the assault on the monarchical establishment.

To read Sade, particularly works such as *Les 120 Journées de Sodome*, a special set of vocabulary is required. In *La Philosophie dans le boudoir*, Eugénie's transparent lexicon is soon filled with physiological terms like, "gorge, seins, tétons," all normal words for the breast, but they are followed by *con* and *motte* ("vagina"), *foutre* ("to copulate"), *vit* ("phallus"), *décharger* ("to have orgasm"), *enculer* ("dorsal" or "anal intercourse"), and so on. Further reading of Sade also requires the use of words like *irrumer* ("to fellate") and *godemiché* ("dildo"). More refined specialties which occur in Mme. de Saint-Ange's boudoir and elsewhere are algolagnia (desire to whip and be whipped), coprophilia (consuming excrement), and necrophilia (fascination with the dead). In contrast, the normal manner of contemplating and denoting pleasure is absent from Sade's vocabulary; no love or mutual satisfaction is present. Dolmancé ordered Eugénie never to use the word *amour* because what she previously understood by the term is corrected as "folly of the mind" (3:503). Monseigneur Chigi states it more bluntly in part 4 of *Juliette:* "I have never believed that from the union of two bodies can there result the union of two hearts. . . . I see nothing more in this physical union than motives for scorn, disgust, but not a single one of love." Roland Barthes noted that Sade frequently refers to the notion of language by the word "imagination,"[9] and indeed we must admit that every conceivable deviation and variation concerning sex is present in the works of Sade.

After identifying La Mettrie and D'Holbach as the forebearers of Sade's system, one more ancestor ought to be added: Rabelais. This colossal humanist partook of almost all the known sciences and arts of his time. His tales of giants, which were the equivalent of our comic books or our widely distributed humor magazines, are a treasure of language and lore. Steeped in Latin and Greek, Rabelais's vocabulary is among the richest in French literature. From a more negative angle, he was also an incorrigible misogynist. In chapter 22 of *Le Tiers Livre*, Rondibilis explains the "terrible animal" inside the female body, which causes women's constant state of turmoil. Hundreds of words are invoked or invented to refer to codpieces, the phallus, and coitus. Sade was quite familiar with Rabelais's works; he even tried to imitate him in his letters to his valet Carteron.[10] But Angela Carter reminds us that there is a vast difference of tone and values between the two. The motto of the utopian abbey of Thélème was "Fais ce que vouldras" ("Do what thou wish"). Rabelais assumed a benevolent and moral clientele for his Thélème, while the inhabitants of Sade's cloisters interpreted the motto as a license for perversion.[11] Joseph McMahon expresses the same view: "Rabelais' gusto creates a world of carnal enthusiasm and innocence; Sade's frenzy replaces the gusto with neurosis and then, in volume after volume, protests that neurosis is good intellectual and physical health, innocence a mirage, the carnal a grotesque fact whose operations are justified by a failure of all efforts to ruin or even reduce its empire."[12] Rabelais's archaic attitudes toward woman could be excused, if not forgiven, by the context and chronological period in which he expressed them. Sade is less forgivable; he was more advanced than some might think. For example, he correctly identified the clitoris as the center of female sexual pleasure. On the other hand, he appeared to have little understanding or notion of ovulation and menstruation. The amphibious Mme. de Saint-Ange will try anything, except when she is menstruating (3:412). The number of myths and inhibitions not shattered by Sade's rogues is small. Sade did not discover perversion, as Eugénie did in *La Philosophie dans le boudoir*. He had no monopoly on liberal sex, as the twentieth century often seems to think it does. He simply surpassed all of his contemporaries in the radical manner of expressing it.

Les 120 Journées de Sodome

If Sade were to be "burned," it would be for *Les 120 Journées de Sodome*. The history of the most important of his philosophically oriented works is as troubled as the events which it narrates. In the last two lines of the manuscript, he tells us: "This entire scroll was begun on 22 October 1785 and completed in thirty-seven days."[13] The manuscript itself is unique. Sade covered both sides of a roll of paper twelve meters in length with minuscule writing. His temporary revisions were completed on 28 November; he then hid the scroll in a gap of his cell wall in the Bastille. According to Lely, the loss of this work in particular caused Sade to shed "tears of blood" in May of 1790, after the destruction of the fortress. [14]

The sinister document survived, however. In 1904, the Berlin psychiatrist Iwan Bloch, using the pseudonym Eugene Duhren, published his version of *Les 120 Journées de Sodome,* citing frequently the similarities between Sade's opus and the case studies in Krafft-Ebing's *Psychopathia sexualis.* The first edition was filled with so many errors that readers doubted its authenticity. In 1929, Maurice Heine obtained the autograph scroll, and published a definitive edition in 1931–35. The notoriety continued. The Pauvert company was tried in 1956 for attempting to publish a limited edition of Sade's works. The decision, rendered two years later, insisted that *Les 120 Journées de Sodome, La Nouvelle Justine,* and *La Philosophie dans le boudoir* be omitted.

The cause for this alarm is as follows. Toward the end of the reign of Louis XIV, four arch-libertines organize a ritual that is to last 120 days. They are all extraordinarily wealthy, and each has a history of vice and crime, including murder. The Duc de Blangis instigates the orgy; like Mme. de Saint-Ange, he enjoys everything; he is a liar, glutton, drunkard, rogue, sodomite, murderer, arsonist, and thief (13:8). His cohorts are the Président de Curval who, like Dolmancé, specialized in anal intercourse; Durcet, a transsexual; and an unnamed but equally corrupt bishop, who killed two orphaned children entrusted to him, after seducing them. Each of the four has a beautiful daughter married to a different member of the quartet: Constance is Durcet's daughter and wife of Blangis; Adelaide, Curval's daughter, married to Durcet; Julie, Blangis's child, wed to Curval; and Aline, illegitimate daughter of the bishop and of Blangis's second wife. To complete the case, notorious pimps and procuresses are hired to kidnap eight virgin girls, eight boys (equally continent), eight "fouteurs" with massive organs, four of the most vile old women available to serve as domestics, six kitchen attendants, and four "historiennes" or storytellers—a total of forty-six. The victims' names are borrowed from classical lore (Narcisse, Hercule, Cupidon), from popular literature or from the street (Giton, Fanny, Thérèse); others bear the names of their physical prowess, for example, Brise-cul and Bande-au-ciel. After a long and complex selection process, and after arrangements for huge quantities of food, drink, costumery, and sexual appliances, the victims are gradually shipped by their masters to the site of the orgy: Durcet's castle of Silling, in the innermost reaches of the Black Forest. Elaborate plans for security have been made; it is physically impossible for an outsider to approach the castle. A temporary access bridge is severed, and the fortress is completely sealed. No trace of an exit is left, and any victim so bold as to attempt an escape is to be executed. Similar to La Coste and Sainte-Marie-des-Bois (*Justine*), no communication with the exterior world is conceivable; the inhabitants are forced to say: "I am alone here, I am at the limit of the world, removed from all eyes, without any creature ever being able to reach me; no restrictions, no barriers" (13:207). As Roland Barthes indicates, the *120 Journées* is not a spontaneous orgy. The group is very structured, with laws and procedures for everything.[15] Any deviation from the prescribed norms is severely punished; the slightest expression of religious belief merits death. Impromptitude or resistance is followed by whipping or mutilation. Even the lords are assessed fines for using one of the victims out of turn. The Rabelaisian "Do what thou wish" of Thélème becomes "Do what is pleasing to me" at Silling (13:57). Of the forty-six people who arrived at Silling in late October, only sixteen, in various stages of destruction, will return to Paris at the end of February. All four of the rogues survive unscathed and unaffected.

Sade is present in his text. The means by which he expressed the innermost reaches of his troubled imagination are four "historiennes," all women whose crimes parallel those of the four organizers. Using a narrative structure somewhat similar to Boccaccio and Marguérite de Navarre, Sade has Madame Duclos narrate the "simple passions" during the month of November; December is reserved for the tales of vice of Madame Champville; La Martaine follows during the third month, then La Desgranges. These notorious women, whose names are derived from their first seducers, have a dais for their speeches, surrounded by and visible to the glass-paneled nests designed for the four rogues and their partners. Sadian vice must be heard as well as seen and acted; discourse plays a fundamental role in the exploration of pleasure: "It is agreed, among true libertines, that the sensations communicated by one's hearing are those which please the most and whose effects are the most vivid" (13:27). If the portrait presented is not adequately detailed, stimulating, or original, one of the four masters intervenes or inflicts punishment.[16]

Since the month of November is the only completed part of *Les 120 Journées de Sodome,* La Duclos's tales are the most developed. The "simple" passions include cases of lecherous priests, masturbation, ingestion of mucus, numerous deflowering rituals, extortion, and a wealth of algolognia. La Champville is responsible for December's entertainment; her experiences include incidents of incest (single and double), and the use of religious objects in sex acts; after 150 items or so, she receives applause. The evening of 24 December and the following day are like all the others: cruelty, rape, and torture. The new year is inaugurated by La Martaine's tales of criminal passions. These are more intense and involve bestiality, phlebotomy, fracturing victims' limbs, amputation, and infanticide as preludes to auto-eroticism. Part 4 completes the horror tale; Desgranges has witnessed or learned of mass murders and tortures, occasionally utilizing elaborate machinery, for example, item 105: "a notoriously incestuous man brings together two sisters; after embuggering them, he ties them to a machine, each with a dagger in hand; the machine is set in motion, the girls approach one another, and thus they kill each other" (13:413).

In retrospect, it is perhaps fortunate for Sade that he was not permitted to finish *Les 120 Journées de Sodome.* The three final parts remain in manuscript form, and each of the new incidents is introduced by an anonymous "Il," personal and impersonal. As for the quantity of crimes, several aspects should be kept in mind. Sade's correspondence and his unedited writings display the continuing fascination for esoteric and complex numerical systems. In the *Journal inédit,* the mania for figures, the counting of days, and the search for numerical keys typify the behavior of a man condemned to what he believed to be perpetual imprisonment. In this regard, Sade was somewhat typical of his age, in the sense that the eighteenth century in France produced a large number of dictionaries, encyclopedias, and catalogs. Also, it is difficult to judge aspects such as style in a work which remained unfinished by its author. Sade's editorial indications are provided in Heine's critical edition; on the one hand, he expressed concern that he had lost control of the work (13:35); on the other, he indicated general satisfaction with his sketch plan. Addressing himself with the formal "vous" pronoun, he wrote in the last pages: "Do not stray in the least from this plan; everything is combined in it, several times over, and with the greatest precision" (13:432). Since part 1 was completed, it does permit an evaluation;

the recitation of La Duclos is neutral, flat, and insensitive. Barring interruption from her master, she tells of one incident after another without transition or logical succession. As was the case in *La Philosophie dans le boudoir,* a brief cue or indication such as "The scene begins, the actors take their positions," is stated summarily, followed by the execution of the scene. As the narrative progresses, human presence and stylistic refinement are further reduced to the cataloging process. One could even say that *Les 120 Journées de Sodome* is an instance of *forme* being identical to the *fond;* the short, staccato, ejaculatory sentences parallel in their expression the mechanical, repeated motions of the actors described.

In writing *Les 120 Journées de Sodome,* Sade had in mind to annotate every possible act or combination of acts of vice. The following remark stands out in his sixty-page introduction:

It is now, my friendly reader, that you must prepare your heart and mind for the most impure narration ever written since the world has existed, no similar book having been written either among the ancients or moderns. . . . Assuredly many of the deviations which you will see portrayed will displease you, we know, but some of them will excite you to the point of making you spill your fuck, and that is all that we need. (13:61).

A more serious indication of the author's point of view and intention in committing to paper these 120 days is found in letter 19 of *Aline et Valcour,* a novel which Sade prepared at the same time as *Les 120 Journées de Sodome* (1785):

I would prefer that all men could have with them. . . a type of tree painted in relief and on each branch there would be written the name of a vice, beginning with the slightest infraction, and gradually moving up to the crime resulting from the neglect of their earliest responsibilities. Would not this moral picture have some use, and would it not be worth as much as a Teniers, or a Rubens?

The resulting "tree" of crime has over six hundred individual acts of debauchery in various stages of completion. All of the graphic language taught to Eugénie de Mistival becomes daily speech in the castle at Silling. Similar to modern authors (Gide, Butor, Robbe-Grillet), Sade had in mind to force his reader into active participation in his text. As he threatened in his introduction, he sought the same degradation of the reader as was given to his characters. Language in Sade is the "jouissance de l'énonciation," as Marcel Hénaff so aptly called it.[17] It is *le dire,* the need to tell all, to account for every conceivable outrage against the male or female body, in defiance of any restraint. But the gradual initiation and stimulation of the "school" of libertinism breaks down, and the pinnacle of the "tree of crime" is barren. On the twelfth day of her private history, Duclos narrates her past encounters with the enthusiasm of a corpse: "And as he pushed his tongue into it (her anus) all the while manipulating himself, the libertine shed his fuck on my legs, not without a multitude of filthy words and curses necessary to complete his ecstasy, so it seemed to me" (13:190).

After reading the Marquis de Sade, we are left with some fundamental notions, as well as some ambiguities. The writer had in mind an encyclopedia of vice, not a bedside book or sex manual. He did not nor could not have done all that he wrote of. He obviously intended to shock his reader, but he was not so bold as to recommend the murder of the victims of his lust. In his "Idée sur les romans," he called for "élans" from other writers: "We want outbursts from you." At the same time, his analysis of fiction prior to 1800 is rather tame. But in *Les 120 Journées de Sodome,* the insistence on and repetition of hedonistic perversion are so intense that even his greatest admirer and defender, Gilbert Lely, was revolted by the emphasis on coprophilia and algolagnia. The reader, like the ghastly survivors of the school of libertinism, is left shocked, alone, and without consolation from the author. But we do participate; we read Sade; we cite his name more than that of any of his contemporaries. We express continuing interest in the millions of victims of the 1940–45 holocaust. Our current vocabulary includes terms such as body count, overkill, and measurements of destruction in megatons. We are intrigued by the accounts of Jack the Ripper, the Boston Strangler, Richard Speck, and the Hillside Strangler. Our media oblige us to an extent, but the media cannot exist without spectators. We remain horrified and fascinated at the same time.

If the literary merit of *Les 120 Journées de Sodome* is dubious (since it was left unfinished), its philosophical implications are quite clear. Certain men in positions of power have limitless rights to any creatures which they might choose. The goal is immediate pleasure and orgasm. The mechanical interpretation of human existence expressed by La Mettrie is echoed in the portrait of Blangis: "he felt that a violent disturbance imposed on any adversary relayed to the cluster of our nerves a vibration whose effect, stimulating the animal instincts which flow into the reservoir of these nerves, compels them to alert the erectional nerves and then produce this quivering known as a lubricous sensation" (13:10). The man-machine association provided a perfect model for the automatic discharges of Blangis, Curval, Durcet, and the bishop. Their consumption of huge quantities of food and liquor aids in the accumulation of sperm. As Vera Lee has astutely noted, Sade's remark to Mlle. Rousset in 1782 is apropos of the orgy-banquet cycle: "There are always two crucial moments in the day which remind man of the sad condition of beasts, and which is not that far removed from our own system: the one when he must fill himself, and the other when he must empty . . ."[18] This process applies to the male sex in most of Sade's works. After all of the praises of sodomy or anal intercourse by Dolmancé, Curval, Almani (in *Juliette*), and others, we find in the castle of Silling a near total disdain for the vagina. Conventional penetration of it is almost never mentioned. To cite only one example, La Martaine's sixty-fifth item discusses the murder of a woman by a libertine who placed her on a platform between a large fire and a deep pool of water. After attempts to save herself from burning and drowning, she perishes; "The libertine, at the sight of this spectacle, masturbates while observing" (13:404). In Sade, the phallus must be stimulated away from the female. If anything, the vagina is befouled, mutilated, or filled with excrement. This disdain does not mean that the Sadian world is exclusively phallocratic, nor that the male organ is always triumphant. On the contrary, those which are described in *Les 120 Journées de Sodome* are more frequently shriveled, dark, and eject sickly droplets of rotted sperm.[19] External physical endowment reflects the internal character of the male libertine.

Sade and Psychology

To fully understand Sade today we must look backward for a moment to the psychologists and theoreticians who had the greatest impact on our current views of him. The first of these is Richard von Krafft-Ebing (1840–1902), who chaired the division of psychology and neurology at the University of Vienna for more than a decade. Krafft-Ebing's *Psychopathia sexualis* (1886) coined the term masochism; it was derived from the name and writings of the German author Sacher-Masoch. *Psychopathia sexualis* consists of more than 200 cases collected from Western European annals and from Krafft-Ebing's own patients, and was used extensively by Freud in his *Three Contributions to the Theory of Sex*.[20] Krafft-Ebing knew Sade's works rather well, certainly better than most of his contemporaries; his judgments were based on the reading of *Justine, Juliette, La Philosophie dans le boudoir,* and on Jules Janin's 1835 biography of Sade. Since Krafft-Ebing expressed the now dubious belief that masturbation was a sign of physical and moral degeneracy, we cannot expect to find a sympathetic treatment of the author of *Justine*. The chapter which deals with sadism in *Psychopathia sexualis* includes an analysis of the career of Jack the Ripper, followed by analogous incidents of lust, murder, mutilation of corpses, defilement of women, whipping of boys, and acts of bestiality. Given the Austrian doctor's limited views, it is unlikely that any knowledge of *Les 120 Journées de Sodome* would have improved his image of Sade. He merely serves as an example of the tendency to associate Sade with criminal sexual behavior.

As opposed to Krafft-Ebing, Freud provided a more logical explanation for the masturbatory and auto-erotic practices in Sade. In the 1905 landmark study entitled *Three Contributions to the Theory of Sex,* Freud devoted several pages to sadism and masochism, following the distinction of Krafft-Ebing (desire to inflict pain versus the desire to be punished, respectively). The treatments of introversion, cruelty, complexes, etc., in Freud's essays bear no specific reference to the Marquis de Sade, however.[21] We must admit that Sade was somewhat more accurate about the nature of female pleasure (clitoral versus vaginal) than the man who completely revised modern psychology. In further defense of Sade, we should recall that his own bisexual inclinations have been understood and scientifically examined only in the past few years. Changes in attitudes and greater understanding help to explain why Sade was sentenced to death for his acts of sodomy in 1772, while his varied acts of perversion with the Marseilles prostitutes caused much less concern.

Sade did not appear to be greatly affected by the other fundamental thesis of Freud, the Oedipus complex or sexual desire of mother by son. If any incestuous tendencies were apparent in his life, they were directed toward his sister-in-law. Jane Gallop points out that in Sade's fiction, the mode of behavior resembles that of Nero more than Oedipus.[22] Nero expressed his desire for his mother by killing her. Such is the case throughout Sade's treatment of mother images.

From the examples quoted earlier, Bressac stands out as the greatest mother hater. His role evolves from that of a homosexual intent on murdering his wealthy aunt in *Justine* to the violator and murderer of his own mother in *La Nouvelle Justine.*

More recent psychological studies on sexuality tend to omit Sade, perhaps because the behavior which he described is no longer considered as deviant as it was formerly. There is nothing about Sade or sadism in either Masters and Johnson's *Human Sexual Response* or Kinsey's works on sexual behavior. There is, however, one instance of clinical psychology in which the Marquis de Sade is discussed. The instance is that of Jacques Lacan (1908–81), founder of the Ecole Freudienne in Paris, and who for many years worked to disseminate the contributions of Freud and to correct prevalent misinterpretations of him. In his 1963 article entitled "Kant avec Sade," Lacan noted the conformity between Sade's philosophical system as expressed in *La Philosophie dans le boudoir* and Kant's *Critique of Practical Reason.* [23] For Kant, man and his behavior are determined by nature and not by any externally imposed system. The moral value of a particular act is derived from the phenomenon or inner attitude of him who commits the act. To this point, the system of Kant coincides with that of Sade, and as expressed by Dolmancé in the treatise "Français, encore un effort si vous voulez être républicains." But beyond the individual determination of morality, Kant is no longer "with" Sade. When Dolmancé proclaims: "I have the right to enjoy your body, I will say to whomever it pleases me, and I shall exercise this right which I prefer to savor to the fullest," the difficulty is that Dolmancé's law of total freedom applies only to the master, and not to the victim. It is not uniquely masculine, since it is valid for Mme. de Saint-Ange, Juliette, and other dominant females. The irreconcilable terminal point of this total freedom for the tormentor versus his constant need of victims culminates in death, if allowed to run its logical course. And death is another major point in Lacan's analysis of Kant and Sade. [24] It may indeed be that the death imposed by the latter on his fictional victims is a second death, in the Freudian sense of death wish. By murder, the aggressor allows himself the "pleasure" of punishing his victim throughout eternity. The paradox or contradiction here is that Sade denied the existence of hell on the one hand, and elevated nature to the level of a deity on the other. [25] His dominant figures are not required to show remorse; as Kant suggested, they may have no

duty other than their immediate and constant gratification; but
their nihilistic, homicidal inclinations cannot be universally justified, either morally or logically.

We should also keep in mind the secret nature of works such as
Les 120 Journées de Sodome. Sade never intended it to be widely distributed as it is today; the publication of far less offensive works
caused enough difficulty for him. But from the works which were
known by his contemporaries, we are assured that what was found
shocking in them was the maximizing of pleasure, in addition to
violence, atheism, and the sheer quantity of crimes. The translation
of Dolmancé's right to "enjoy" others is based on the French verb
jouir, which signifies both asexual and orgasmic enjoyment, both
in Sade's time and today. La Mettrie composed an *Art de jouir:* he
recognized the presence of sexual extremes and cruelty, but without
praising them.[26] According to Roger Lacombe, Sade also wrote an
Art de jouir, which has been lost.[27] Whatever its contents may have
been, we can infer that the same pursuit of unbridled lust would
have been found in it. Sade's *Juliette* was to carry this search of *la
jouissance complète* to the far corners of the world.

Chapter Three
The *Justine* Cycle

Justine

Justine, ou les Malheurs de la vertu is without doubt Sade's masterpiece. He wrote it while in the Bastille in the 1785–88 period, and published it in 1791.[1] In spite of frequent denials of authorship, we know that indeed Sade wrote it; it was mentioned in his *Catalogue raisonné*, a list of works completed by October 1788. And in 1791, he wrote to Reinaud (a lawyer in Aix): "They are currently printing a novel of mine, but it is too immoral to be sent to a man as proud and as decent as you. I needed money, my publisher requested that I spice it up, and so I did, enough to arouse the devil. It is called *Justine, ou les Malheurs de la vertu*. Burn it, do not read it if you should happen upon it. I deny it . . ." (2:478). Six editions of *Justine* were printed in ten years. And since it was the first of Sade's works published during his lifetime, it played a very important role in determining his reputation at the time. The reactions were not necessarily favorable, however; if anything, they decried its immorality and infamy. In October 1799 the journal *L'Ami des lois* denounced Sade as the "infamous author of the atrocious *Justine*" (2:467). In attacking *Les Liaisons dangereuses*, the *Tribunal d'Apollon* stated that Laclos's novel was the only recent work equal to the "infamous *Justine*," from the points of view of criminality and the high number of victims (2:467). When Inspector Colins visited the Charenton asylum in 1812, he was shocked by the fact that the author of the "infamous novel *Justine*" was given permission to direct plays and use the inmates of Charenton for his casts.[2] Rétif de la Bretonne, who loathed Sade apparently as much as Sade loathed him, claimed that the fair sex was so endangered by Sade's *Justine* and *La Nouvelle Justine* that he felt compelled to write his *Anti-Justine* in defense of women. Rétif argued that by using the same medium that he criticized in Sade (pornography), he would cause his male readers to become so stimulated that they would rush home

41

to their wives for satisfaction, and avoid immoral works sold on the streets.[3]

The association of Sade with *Justine* continued throughout the first decades of the nineteenth century, as did his reputation of immorality. Michaud's *Biographie universelle* (1854 edition) maintained this image, with its identification of *Aline et Valcour* and *Justine* as "two infamous productions." The rest of Sade's works received similar judgments in the entry. Criticism aside, Sade was sufficiently intrigued with his *Justine* story to have expanded it over a period of ten years and to have created three distinct versions of it.

The principal version of *Justine*, but not necessarily the most infamous one, can be summarized as follows. Two sisters, Juliette and Justine, are orphaned at an early age, left penniless, and expelled from the convent school which sheltered them. Whereas Juliette uses her charms and skills to become wealthy and successful (much more will be said of her skills), Justine becomes the epitome of a *souffre-douleur*. Justine has already lived the adventures which she narrates to her sister and uses the name Thérèse during that narration. Her first encounter is with a wicked priest who attempts to seduce her instead of giving her the charitable assistance which she sought. She also tells of her experience with the financier Dubourg; he abuses her and forces her to commit robbery. Dubourg will be rewarded for his vice by a lucrative government appointment. Then Justine passes on to the service of Du Harpin, an expert in usury, who plots the robbery of a neighbor, using Justine as an intermediary. Arrested and imprisoned as a cruel result of Du Harpin's false charges, Justine is freed by a woman named Dubois, who engineers their escape by setting fire to the prison. The two fugitives meet up with Dubois's brigand friends, led by Coeur-de-fer. Justine is sexually mistreated by the gang of robbers during the intervals in which she is not participating in their raids. One of their crimes is the robbery and beating of Saint-Florent, whom Justine helps to escape; he expresses his gratitude by raping her and taking the little money which she had.

Abandoned and distraught in a woods, Justine happens upon a young count, Bressac, in the midst of a homosexual act with a servant. Instead of killing her then and there for her indiscretion, Bressac takes her home and forces her into assisting in his project to murder his wealthy aunt. After four years with Bressac, Justine flees and is hired by Rodin, supposedly a surgeon, but more accurately a vivisector, who practices his art on his daughter (Rosalie) and on young children. Justine's attempt to rescue Rosalie fails; Justine is caught and branded on the rear as a common criminal.

Similar to the device used in *Les 120 Journées de Sodome*, Justine contains an isolated citadel of vice: Sainte-Marie-des-bois. It is operated by four roguish monks: Severino, Clément, Jérôme, and Antonin. Like Blangis's castle at Silling, the abbey is completely isolated; it contains human stables for the practice of various excesses, according to the age, sex, and charms of the prisoners. Justine does escape from Sainte-Marie-des-bois, but only after participating in the wildest of orgies.

In part 2, Justine is taken in by Gernande, a lecherous glutton whose specialty is phlebotomy (blood-letting) as a prelude to sexual excitement. Gernande has already killed three wives in this manner, and his fourth spouse is near death as a result of the same practice. When fate allows an opportunity to escape, Justine does so; she meets Saint-Florent again, now a slaver trafficking in children. Her next captor is Roland, a notorious counterfeiter, who uses only women to turn the wheels of his machinery and who tortures or murders them if they should attempt an escape. The cycle of one misfortune after another continues, with a single brief pause. When the counterfeiting operation is seized, Justine is defended by one sympathetic male figure (but without a name), monsieur S***. Shortly thereafter, Dubois returns and incriminates Justine in a poisoning in Grenoble. In Lyons, Justine attempts to rescue a friend's child from a burning building, only to be accused of arson and robbery by the despairing mother. The monk Antonin reappears, but rejects Justine's appeal for help. Saint-Florent also returns, but turns her over to a group of sodomites for use in their orgy.

At this point, the condemned Justine summarizes her woes and apologizes to her sister and to M. de Corville for having offended them by the recitation of her sufferings. She is at last recognized as Justine, the lost sister of Juliette; the accusations and sentences against her are cleared by Corville's interventions. But, as one might expect from her past adventures, happiness is short-lived: during a storm, Justine is struck by a lightning bolt which completely disfigures her before killing her. Such is Sade's last ghastly evidence against the expectation of reward for virtue.

From the structures of *Les 120 Journées de Sodome* and *La Philosophie dans le boudoir,* we know that Sade's arch-libertines are not contented with merely acting out their fantasies; they must also discourse on them. This is equally true of the major villains encountered by Justine. Dubourg attempts to make clear to Justine the value of moral behavior: "This virtue which you flaunt so freely is of no use whatsoever in the world" (3:68). The same idea is repeated more intensely by Rodin and Roland. Coeur-de-fer praises sodomy, as does Bressac. When Justine wonders why Saint-Florent rewarded her kindness with cruelty, he digresses on the futility of seeking assistance from God. The idea is carried a step further in Sainte-Marie-des-bois, where Clément speculates that man is predisposed toward evil, thus justifying uninterrupted debauchery. In view of his penchant for bleeding women, it comes as no surprise that Gernande expounds on misogyny. After all the horrors experienced by Justine, Dubois asks her: "What proves to you that this providence loves order and by that, virtue? Has it not given you endless examples of its injustice and inconsistency?" (3:297). Justine's reaction to the question is as predictable as the other evidence against virtue rewarded. She is not intended to acquire wisdom, as would normally be the case in a *bildungsroman;* all that she can do is to pose another feeble question. She is a thing, a means to the end of demonstration that one good turn does not deserve another.

The Other Versions of *Justine*

The earliest version of *Justine* was written in fifteen days in 1787 while Sade was in the Bastille prison. The manuscript was found by Guillaume Apollinaire in 1909 and grouped among the "Nouvelles Acquisitions françaises" in the Bibliothèque nationale. This was the text used by Maurice Heine to publish *Les Infortunes de la vertu* in 1930.[4] From the scant documentation which has survived, we can assume that Sade considered the subtitle of *Justine,* that is, *Les Malheurs de la vertu,* as the principal title for the earlier version; he then substituted *Les Infortunes de la vertu* as the definitive one. Also in the earlier version, the heroine is called Sophie, like the girl believed to be the lost sister of Aline in *Aline et Valcour.* As will be explained further, *Les Infortunes de la vertu* is much shorter than *Justine;* the several encounters with Saint-Florent are absent in the earlier rendition; the Gernande episode is completely absent, and the philosophical digressions are considerably shorter. Among the minor changes, the name of one of the four monks in the Benedictine abbey is changed (Raphael instead of Severino), and a certain Dalville is the leader of the counterfeiting operation, instead of Roland, who merely succeeds him. With these exceptions stated, the basic narrative remains intact, including the final destruction.

After the *succès de scandale* occasioned by the publication of *Justine* in 1791, Sade returned to his masterpiece and expanded it into *La Nouvelle Justine* (printed in 1797). The sheer length of each of the three renditions indicates the amount of work and interest of the author. *Les Infortunes de la vertu* contains only 130 pages (in the Tête de Feuilles edition used in this study); *Justine* comprises about 300 pages, or more than twice the length of the first form; this amount was again redoubled in the 810-page *Nouvelle Justine*. The *Juliette* story, which constitutes the sequel to *La Nouvelle Justine,* is the longest of all, with more than 1,100 pages in the edition used here.

Béatrice Didier provides an indication as to how the transformation was effected. In 1926, Maurice Heine discovered the manuscript of the last version of the tale, *La Nouvelle Justine.* Attached to the pages of this manuscript were overleafs which contained the additions and amplifications to the novel of 1791 (*Justine*).[5] Therefore Sade had the principal account in front of him and, with ample time for reflection, added material and episodes. The same must be said for the change from *Les Infortunes de la vertu* to *Justine,* since many of the passages in each are identical.

Yet vast differences are apparent in the 1791 and 1797 forms of the *Justine* story. *La Nouvelle Justine* is narrated in the third person, as opposed to the *je.* Thus it can give the impression of being more impersonal and distant. Sade added numerous characters to this longer form. Dubourg acquires a friend and accomplice, Delmonse. A child-killer named Bandole is included between the Rodin episode and that of Sainte-Marie-des-bois. Two additional monks are on the abbey's staff (Ambroise and Sylvestre). A libertine named D'Esterval is introduced in the second half of the work; he and his wife rob and murder the guests who happen by their inn. This illustrious family serves as the means to interrelate Gernande, Bressac, Verneuil, and others into one large corrupt family. Finally, an archbishop of Grenoble is created to expound on a political system which, by infanticide and pederasty, would alleviate the problem of overpopulation (7:363–70). A few changes involve the characters already present in the 1791 edition of *Justine*. In *La Nouvelle Justine*, Saint-Florent becomes a voyeur, not just an ingrate. Bressac plots to kill not his aunt, but his mother (a scheme reminiscent of *La Philosophie dans le boudoir*). Rodin has a new co-conspirator, his sister. As might be expected, the philosophical digressions are more numerous and lengthier. Brother Jérôme, for instance, narrates his entire career in lechery for more than eighty pages.

Beyond the preceding distinctions in basic plot patterns from *Les Infortunes* to *La Nouvelle Justine*, one must add the differences of tone, language, and violence depicted. Béatrice Didier notes appropriately the increased emphasis on incest, lesbianism, coprology, and mechanical torture in the 1797 edition.[6] Most of the principal tableaux lend themselves to a comparative study in this process of increased violence. Taking the scene of Justine and her encounter with Coeur-de-fer and his brigands, we note first that the episode occupies only five pages in *Les Infortunes de la vertu* (14:352–57). Justine-Sophie is tempting to them, and they push and shove one another to see who will be the first to approach her. But while Dubois tries to separate them, the heroine has enough time to flee without being violated. In *Justine*, the title character is forced to join the gang; Dubois attempts to protect her but fails, and Thérèse is abused by all four villains:

The second one forced me onto my knees between his legs, and while Dubois satisfied him and the other men, two other procedures occupied this one; he alternately slapped me with an open hand, a rather nervous hand, either on my cheeks or breast; at the same time, his impure mouth explored my own. My neck and face instantly became scarlet red. . . . (3:84)

A vivid imagination is not required to infer what will take place in the rest of the scene, in spite of innocuous words such as "satisfied, occupied, explored," etc. But everything is not bluntly stated, as is the case in *La Nouvelle Justine*.

The same episode with the brigands in *Justine* lasts for thirteen pages. In *La Nouvelle Justine*, it includes more than thirty pages. The increase is accounted for in part by a long speech by Coeur-de-fer and by details of the humiliations imposed on Justine by each of the criminals, in terms vastly more explicit than in the earlier versions:

Get into position, said Coeur-de-fer. My sister, go stretch out on that bed; Brise-Barre will fuck you. Justine will straddle Dubois, put her cunt in Brise-Barre's face, and will piss in his mouth; I know what his likes are.

—Oh! fuck, said the rogue, in adapting himself to Dubois's cunt, that is my greatest delight, and I thank you for having suggested it. He fucks, pisses, and discharges, then Sans-Quartier goes to work. (4:134–35)

It is easy to see that by this time (1797) any inhibitions or limitations in Sade's zest for lewdness have been forgotten, and that the new *Justine* is much more akin to *Juliette* than to the preceding versions of the same story.

Alice Laborde has concentrated on the same evolution of Justine's story from *Les Infortunes* to *La Nouvelle Justine*.[7] Using the episode of the abbey at Sainte-Marie-des-bois as her specimen, Laborde notes first that this scene increased almost tenfold from the first to the final edition. Laborde also points out that the two earlier texts are "commémoratifs," that is, they provide a mimesis of a reality; they are more plausible and follow an approximate chronological order. *La Nouvelle Justine* is, however, so long and so violent that it is more similar to *Juliette* and its system of initiation. Laborde's juxtaposition and analysis of the three forms of the abbey scene is the best account to date of the evolution from the relatively tame story of 1787 to the scathing edition of ten years later.

Assuming that *Les Infortunes* was primarily the draft for *Justine* and not intended for publication, the question may still be asked as to why the author took a basically coherent and somewhat clean story and stretched it into a scandalous tale of horror more than twice as long. Several answers are possible. For Sade to pay so much attention to the *Justine* cycle reveals an element of satisfaction with it; he knew that he had written a masterpiece. Obviously, he also had a great deal of time to dispose of, and he was so taken with portions such as the abbey episode that he wrote four or five drafts of it. In 1797, when he was at last free to walk in the streets of Paris, he was in such desperate need of money (as he constantly repeated to his correspondents of that period) that the progressive degradation of *Justine* would have been a means of selling more copies; given his dire financial condition, he could hardly refuse a publisher who requested more "spice" in the story. Public moral standards may have been more relaxed after 1791, but as Didier reminds us, the new republican government was at least outwardly committed to the cult of virtue,[8] and thus Sade's arrest by the man who saw himself as the preserver of the Revolution (Napoleon) comes as no surprise.

Theme and Technique

The message intended to be shared by an author with his or her reader could not be more obvious than in *Justine*. It is visible in the subtitle, the "Misfortunes of Virtue"; it is the only conclusion to be drawn from each of the dozen main episodes. All other characters remind Justine of it constantly, and it is stressed in Sade's introduction: "The purpose of this novel (not so much a novel as one might think) is assuredly new: the ascendancy of virtue over vice, the rewarding of good, the punishment of evil, such is the customary operation of works of this nature; have we not had enough of it?" (3:51). This reversal of the usual moralizing or didactic point of view by which virtue is always recompensed and vice punished is one of Sade's innovations. Most of the French novels prior to his were consistent in the punishment of evil: anarchy and destruction in both France and Persia in *Les Lettres persanes;* the death of the prostitute heroine in *Manon Lescaut;* separation, exile, and marriage to someone else in *La Nouvelle Héloïse;* death for both villains in *Les Liaisons dangereuses,* to name but a few. As he stated often and adamantly, Sade was not interested in such conventions.

In regard to precedents or models for *Justine,* Matthew Lewis's Ambrosio in *The Monk* (1796) is frequently cited; but Lewis's monk is by no means as sinister nor as promiscuous as Sade's benedictines. The date of appearance of *Justine* (1791) and Sade's lack of familiarity with English preclude influence by Lewis. He also praised Mrs. (Ann) Radcliffe in his "Idée sur les romans" in 1800, but her most important works, *The Romance of the Forest* (1791), *The Mysteries of Udolpho* (1794), and *The Italian* (1795), however similar to Sade's "gothic" features, appeared too late to have influenced the *Justine* cycle. I must agree with Jean Fabre in excluding the possibility of direct influence from England in Sade's best known works.[9] As was mentioned earlier, however, Sade had an ample library, and was a devotee of Northern literature.[10]

If there was an immediate precedent for *Justine* in French literature, it might have been Voltaire's *Candide.* All three versions of

Sade's *Justine* begin with an appropriate reference to *Zadig:* there is no evil from which some good does not result, and consequently men should do evil as much as it suits them, since it is merely one more way of doing good (*Zadig,* chap. 18). Sade's interpretation of *Zadig* is slightly Panglossian, but as we already know, he had a good knowledge of Voltaire's works, and adapted them to suit his own purposes. In "L'Idée sur les romans," he qualified both *Zadig* and *Candide* as "pure masterpieces."

The narrative structure of *Candide* resembles a zigzag line, that is to say, a series of rebounds between good and bad fortune: bliss in the baron's castle, followed immediately by expulsion and war; the return of Pangloss, the Lisbon earthquake; Candide's rediscovery of Cunégonde, only to lose her, and so on. The plot line of *Justine* is more horizontal in its depiction of apparently unrelated misfortunes. When Candide is abused, he is at least forceful enough to ask the question: could the blind philosophy of optimism be a futile one? Justine never questions, she merely submits. Both Sade and Voltaire attack the corruption of clerics (with different reasons); both texts contain a high percentage of evildoing, and both depict women unfavorably, but with major differences of extent and of motivation. More importantly, *Candide* and *Justine* present a Manichean view of the world, according to which human life is caught up in a power struggle between the forces of good and evil. When Candide protests: "There are no more Manicheans in the world," Martin replies: "There is me" (chap. 20). This Manichean viewpoint in *Justine* is best expressed by the bandit Coeur-de-fer, for whom men are in a perpetual state of war with one another:

It is not virtue which maintains our criminal associations; it is self-interest and egotism; hence this praise of virtue that you drew from some ephemeral hypothesis is disproved; I suspect that it is not by virtue that, believing myself to be the strongest of the gang, that I do not stab my comrades, because then I would be alone and deprive myself of the fortunes which I could obtain through their help. . . . But, you might say, a perpetual state of war may result. So be it! Is this not the law of nature, the only one which is truly appropriate for us? (3:92–93)

Most of the other villains whom Justine meets rationalize their misdeeds with comparably defiant statements. Whereas in *Candide* at least one erroneous sytem is repudiated, vice and crime triumph from one end to the other of *Justine.* At the conclusion of *Candide,*

Voltaire offers a modest vegetable garden, neither optimistic or pessimistic, but a practical means of forgetting the insoluble problems which beset humans. For all her efforts to resist vice, Justine receives a fatal bolt of lightning from the heavens.

The characters in *Candide* have neither depth nor credibility. We do not choose to "identify with" Candide; as for Cunégonde, we are told that she is, at least in the beginning, "fresh, plump, and appetizing" and later becomes dark and wrinkled. The same is true of Justine who, as both Didier and Miller remind us, is even less credible.[11] A few references to the heroine's age, dress, (or lack of it) and charms are given, but characterization is completely subordinated to the expression of theme, and to that which Sade sarcastically names the "masterpiece of philosophy" in his introduction. Justine is not Sade's spokesman; on the contrary, she is a pawn, abused and humiliated in a series of acts of aggression. She is static and irremedial. After unspeakable mistreatment in suspicious places, she willingly accompanies Roland to his den, "because I could not suppress the extreme desire which I felt to approach this man and to give him my assistance" (3:266). Moments later, she becomes his slave.

Historians of eighteenth-century French prose have difficulties in classifying Voltaire's *Romans et contes* which includes the longer *Candide* and *Zadig,* and the much shorter *Micromégas, Le Monde comme il va,* etc. In the case of Sade, is *Les Infortunes de la vertu* a *conte* because of its shortness, and *La Nouvelle Justine* a novel, because of its length of more than 1,000 pages? And *Justine?* According to Barry Ivker, *Justine* is a *conte philosophique.*[12] In contrast, Didier and most other critics treat it as a *roman* (usually translated as novel). And from the first to the last version of Sade's work, Didier identifies a metamorphosis from the *conte* to the *roman romantique noir.*[13] The criterion of length does not in itself provide much of a solution; content is more important. We know that the *conte* is something specific when used by Voltaire. Sade himself did not appear to be preoccupied with the question of genre; in his *Catalogue raisonné* of 1788 he qualified *Justine* as a work which was completely new, but only in the sense that "From one end to another, vice triumphs and virtue is humiliated" (3:270). Genre is therefore subordinated to message. *Justine* has a style, like any major work; it is a predictable one, with little discernment of individual modes of discourse among the speakers. The longer philosophical digressions are equally uniform, with exception allowed for contextual vocabulary and pseudohistorical references. During one such instance, Gernande's eight-page digression on misogyny (3:246–53), Justine can interpose only one line: "Oh! sir, I said to him, your conversion [to righteousness] is impossible" (3:251). Justine's own style consists of an occasional exclamation or interjection, and she is allowed little else. Sade is not a master of suspense: the string of encounters followed by misfortune becomes blatantly predictable. But his *Justine* stands apart from the long pontifications of *Les 120 Journées de Sodome* and *Juliette*. He was aware that he had created something unique with *Justine,* in spite of the chronological proximity to those other works, and he emphasized this uniqueness by adding: "Would it not be better to say to these noble rivals: we also know how to create."[14]

In the first two chapters of this study, the notion of pornography was briefly examined, with mention of the fact that the French look upon it rather as an "offense against public morality," without precisely defining pornography. It was also mentioned that, in 1801, Sade was arrested with his publisher, and editions of *La Nouvelle Justine* and *Juliette* were confiscated. The *Justine* of 1791 is extreme when compared to other French fiction of the same era, but not categorically pornographic, for reasons explained above. Other writers of the period confronted or identified with the problem of pornography were Crébillon *fils,* Diderot, and Fougeret de Montbron. In 1742, Crébillon *fils* was banished from the Paris region for having written *Le Sopha,* in which the furniture piece referred to in the title "spoke" and revealed the most intimate aspects of the lives of the women who reclined on it. Diderot earned a stay in the Bastille for his *Bijoux indiscrets,* even more insipid than *Le Sopha,* but similar in the device utilized. The "jewels" were the vaginas of Mangogul's courtesans, who "spoke" indiscreetly when a magic ring was turned toward them. In both cases, the language employed is quite prudent when compared to Sade's scatology, except for several bawdy passages in *Les Bijoux indiscrets;* but even these were converted into "foreign" languages.

In discussions of eighteenth-century pornography, Fougeret de Montbron's *Margot la ravaudeuse* (1750) is frequently cited, and only here do we find some genuine resemblance with *Justine.* In a rather typical scene involving Margot's experience with a monk, no more or less of the graphic details found in Sade are involved:

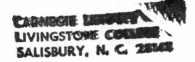

As soon as he had positioned me where it suited him, he raised his coat up over his legs, and withdrew from his leather pants the most handsome, the most superb piece . . . .; in short, an engine more befitting a pair of royal breeches than the disgusting and filthy pants of a sickly soldier in the order of Saint Francis. I felt that Priapus [god of virility] and all of his followers were entering my body. The intense pain which I felt at the insertion of this monster, however venerable, caused me to emit such loud yells, that I feared that I might cause a general alarm in the vicinity. However, the pain was soon forgotten by the delicious agonies into which I fell.[15]

We are all aware, in spite of the opaqueness of the words used, of what has happened, and we have witnessed similarly veiled episodes in passages taken from *Justine.* By neoclassical standards, both of these works were considered "infamous" and pornographic, and were certainly offensive. But when compared to twentieth-century standards of decency and indecency, they may not seem quite so shocking.

At the end of *La Nouvelle Justine,* the narrator promises that the adventures of Juliette, Justine's sister, will appear soon, and instead of the dreary "misfortunes of virtue," the reader will be able to delight in the "prosperities of vice." The dichotomy is no mere coincidence. As Blanchot reminds us, everything which happens to Justine will also happen to Juliette, but while the former anguishes, Juliette will come alive and revel in prisons, torture scenes, and crime.[16]

Juliette

In all three versions of *Justine,* the unfortunate heroine is supposedly recounting her experiences to her as yet unidentified sister Juliette. The latter, instead of submitting and suffering, puts her time and talent to more profitable and more enjoyable use. The details of those lost years constitute the epic fantasy *Juliette,* published in 1797. *Juliette* is to *Justine* what *Les 120 Journées de Sodome* is to *La Philosophie dans le boudoir* from the point of view of intensity. Considered from another angle, Juliette is an adult version of Eugénie de Mistival, having had the time to grow up and put to use the libertine principles instilled in her.[17]

A thorough synopsis of this work is unnecessary. To the reader of Sade's philosophical tracts and the *Justine* story, many of its features will seem routine. Therefore, to mention only the newer and more unique features of *Juliette,* we should begin with her first mentor, Mme. Delbène, who introduces her disciple to the pleasures of inflicting pain on others, and the joys of group sex. Juliette is supposedly an adolescent, but shows no juvenile modesty or reluctance to experience sex. Delbène's final lesson to her pupil is: "Oh my friend, fuck, you were born to fuck! Nature created you to be fucked" (8:90). After leaving Delbène's school, Juliette meets Mme. de Lorsange (wife of Juliette's future husband) who initiates her into the fine art of theft, as a supplement to carnal pleasure. Juliette will become a skilled thief by robbing Minski, Albani, and Noirceuil, among others. These actions are antithetical, one might at least say, to her sister Justine's experience with a beggar, who robbed Justine of her entire purse, instead of just accepting her generous offer of alms (*Justine,* 3:264).

Among the most notorious villains in *Juliette,* we must mention Noirceuil, Saint-Fond, and Minski. The first of these expounds to Juliette on his belief in man's duality, and the mutual attraction of virtue and vice (8:142–57). Noirceuil feels total independence, without obligations to anyone. To support his thesis of immorality, he provides a typical Sadian "lesson" which traces the absence of morality throughout antiquity, civilized and uncivilized nations (8:178–89). At the end, he arranges a transvestite wedding: both he and Juliette marry two people of the opposite sex on the same day, but he as a bride and she as a groom (9:569–70). Thereafter he will violate Juliette's seven-year-old daughter, and then roast her alive, with the mother's permission. The book concludes with his appointment to a high-ranking ministerial post.

Saint-Fond exerts the greatest amount of control in Juliette's life. A minister also, and the king's favorite, he becomes tremendously wealthy by stealing from the royal treasuries. He proposes a series of universal reforms which include the abolishment of religion, enslavement of the masses, freedom to commit murder, incest, rape, sodomy, and so on (8:309–10). His personal ideas are directly reflected in the rules for the "Society of Friends of Crime," which Juliette eagerly waits to join. Like any other charter group, this society has among its forty-five bylaws, rules giving the conditions of eligibility, dues, facilities, attendance, and elections. Number 40 summarizes the others quite adequately: "Comfort, liberty, impurity, crapulence, all the excesses of libertinism, all those of debauchery and gluttony, and, in short, all which are called filth and

pleasure will majestically reign over this assembly" (8:407). As an
example of the spontaneous and graphic language of Juliette, I quote
her answers to the frank questions asked during her initiation into
the Society:

> —Are you married?
> —No.
> —Are you a virgin?
> —No.
> —Have you been embuggered?
> —Often.
> —Fucked in the mouth?
> —Frequently.
> —Whipped?
> —A few times.
> —What is your name?
> —Juliette.
> —What is your age?
> —Eighteen.
> —Have you masturbated with women?
> —Often.
> —Have you ever committed crimes?
> —Several.
> —Did you ever try to kill anyone?
> —Yes.
> —Do you promise to forever live in the same degeneracy?
> —I swear it.

(At this point renewed applause could be heard.) (8:412)

After correctly answering other direct questions as to her sexual
diversifications and their frequency, Juliette is initiated into the
Society. Actions in *Juliette* are as spontaneous and frank as words.
In Italy, Juliette and her friend Durand take on fifty sailors in the
port of Venice, simply because they have several free hours of which
to dispose (9:441).

Minski is one of Sade's more imaginative creations. Of Russian descent, aged forty-five, over seven feet tall, with a penis eighteen inches in length and sixteen in circumference, he maintains a stable of several hundred girls whom he devours after impaling them. When Juliette fears that he may be a danger to her own life, she attempts to poison him; the dosage is too weak, the ogre recovers, but not before Juliette has had time to flee to Italy.

Among the libertines whom she meets in Italy, there are Leopold, who specializes in killing the children of Florence, Princess Olympe Borghese of Rome, whom Juliette pushes into the crater of Mount Vesuvius simply because she "bored" her (9:416), the corrupt King Ferdinand and Queen Charlotte of Naples, and Brisa-Testa (also known as Borchamps), who narrates at length his travels and crimes in Sweden and Russia (9:219, 312); these include an orgy with the Russian empress Catherine. The highlight of this incredible trip through Italy must be Juliette's ordeal with Braschi, a murderer who also happens to be Pope Pius VI. After providing a history of papal corruption and another one in defense of murder, he and Juliette copulate on the central altar of St. Peter's basilica.

Apart from the wilder exaggerations, Sade had some authoritative basis for speaking about Italy. He had traveled there twice (in 1772 and 1775), and his *Voyage d'Italie* is a rather objective account of those travels. In conformity with the type of people whom Juliette encountered, Sade commented on the depravity of Florence and Naples and the decline of Rome, as Du Bellay, Montaigne, and other French travelers had noted. He also listed and described buildings, monuments, and works of art that interested him. Among these, he expressed keen interest in erotic art, for example, a statue of a hermaphrodite in Florence (16:156), another similar statue in Rome (210), and many paintings and sculptures of nudes. Accordingly, Ferdinand serves as Juliette's guide on a tour of the treasures of Florence, and she is especially aroused by the *Venus de Medicis,* the *Hermaphrodite,* and *Caligula caressing his sister* (16:22–24). Sade's travelogue of 1775 is on the whole straightforward narrative, but he was able to incorporate large portions of it to add an epic dimension to *Juliette,* and thereby add something different and dignified to an otherwise pornographic work.

Sade did not forget that Juliette was supposed to be the sister of Justine. If we recall the earlier work, the two young girls had been orphaned. Near the end of part 1 of *Juliette,* the orphans' "real"

father returns, identifies himself as Bernole, explains that since he
and their mother were cousins and that their families were opposed
to such a marriage, they were forced to separate, and tells Juliette
that her mother was killed by a certain Noirceuil (Juliette's present
companion in vice). Instead of offering him the help which he seeks,
Juliette seduces Bernole; after having dorsal intercourse with her
father, she murders him (8:446–54). This minor incident further
reveals the vast difference in tone between *Justine* and the adventures
of her sister.

While escapading through much of the known world, Juliette
refines her skill as a thief and, as seen in the treatment of her father,
she also becomes an adept murderer. This crime receives more emphasis than any other in the work. In *Sexual Politics,* Kate Millet
observes: "All sadistic pornography tends to find its perfection in
murder."[18] Citing examples from D. H. Lawrence, Henry Miller,
Norman Mailer, and Jean Genêt, Millet discerns a trend toward the
practice called "death-fuck," by which the violence exerted against
a female either symbolically or literally results in her death. Although Millet did not have Sade in mind specifically, the practice
had to have been latent in Sade's personal instances of sexual aggression (whipping, binding, cutting), and could not be more evident
than in *Juliette.* It was mentioned that in *Justine,* the closer Gernande's wife approached death by bleeding, the more intense was
his orgasm. The same is true of Rodin, who delights in hanging
his victims to the point of asphyxiation, and who has the same thing
done to himself. After Juliette and Olympe murder a Roman named
Grillo and his wife simultaneously, the heroine gloats: "I will not
describe for you the ecstasy which this scene gave Borghese and me;
while both of us were frigged by Dolni, we had at least ten orgasms
in a row, and this atrocity, I must confess, is among those whose
sharp points have warmed my blood the longest and set constant
fire to my senses" (9:128–29). Also, Juliette's "pope" is an unbridled
misanthropist and murderer. As for the others, Saint-Fond kills an
entire family, for the sheer pleasure of watching them die (8:352).
A woman named Durand is an expert with poisons; at the end of
the novel, she returns to France, as did Juliette, but not before
causing the deaths of 20,000 Venetians through an epidemic (9:584).
Similarly, Noirceuil and Juliette poison a village well, killing its
1,500 inhabitants (9:581–82). While other Sadian philosophers (the
dying man, Dolmancé, Coeur-de-fer) contented themselves for the

most part with speculation on the pleasures derived from murder, it becomes routine practice in *Juliette*. The central female character represents the limit of Sade's imagination concerning sexual profligacy, and murder constitutes the limit of his aggressive tendency. In later novels and short stories, this extremism will diminish, since one can go no further in violence than mass destruction.

Perhaps the best differentiation of Sade's two "sisters" was written by Guillaume Apollinaire who, we recall, was instrumental in making Sade known to the public in the first part of this century. Apollinaire observed: "Justine is the old woman, subjugated, miserable, and less than human; Juliette, on the contrary, represents the new woman he glimpses, a being we cannot conceive of, that breaks loose from humanity, that will have wings and will renew the universe."[19] The freedom realized by Juliette, together with the earlier reference to Kate Millet, calls for some general observations on the treatment of women by Sade and the treatment of Sade by women critics. We have already seen that heterosexual love in Sade's works is exceptional, if not totally absent, and that women are merely the object of male aggression. More often than not, the vagina is neglected in favor of other orifices. When Durand is approached by a young man for the purpose of conventional sex, she protests: "Why would you expect this horrible thing of me? I do not like to fuck in the cunt; I cannot, moreover; what do you take me for, an ordinary woman?" (*Juliette,* 8:513).

If women have no sexual dignity in Sade, we could also say that they have no physical identity. Justine and Juliette exist only in terms of their relationship to males.[20] Furthermore, women have no civil or monetary rights. If Juliette becomes temporarily rich from theft and other crimes, she remains under the control of Noirceuil and Saint-Fond. It seems that Sade envisaged two types of women. They are either prostitutes condemned to wander the streets and be picked up for use by wealthy males; there were many of these in Sade's life, and the professional whores such as Dubois and Durand aptly typify them. Or, women can be enslaved by men and submit to eventual murder. The practices of Roland, Rodin, and Minski demonstrate this latter image of women. Juliette may be freer than the other females in Sade, but she must continually rob and kill in order to survive.

For the Sade system to work, the male aggressors must have total impunity, and here the successes of Gernande (*Justine*) and Saint-

Fond (*Juliette*) provide the best examples. Crime does pay in these works, and it pays well, with lucrative political rewards to accompany the monetary gains. To commit his acts of violence against others, the Sadian male requires total isolation. Here, we should recall the sealed doors and guarded recesses of Sainte-Marie-des-bois and the meeting place of the Society of Friends of Crime. Béatrice Didier has written a compelling thesis concerning the "château intérieur" in Sade; she notes that his fictional châteaux are always described from the interior, which corresponds to man's inner feelings and desires, and that the exterior appearance is completely neglected.[21] After Sade's long periods of incarceration, the theme of claustration becomes inseparable from his writings. To this notion we should add that Sade's manor at La Coste served as the laboratory for his most secret libertine practices until his arrest and the confiscation of his property forced him to create other isolated fortresses in fiction.

In view of the extreme abuse by Sade of women, it comes as no surprise that women critics feel a need to express an opinion on the Marquis de Sade. Simone de Beauvoir was one of the first to do so. Her 1955 essay, *Faut-il brûler Sade?*, is more sympathetic to him than one might have expected, but establishes some fundamental points, for example, the public nature of Sadian wantonness and the one-sided nature of libertine pleasure. Many other women authors treat the phenomenon of sadism, as psychologists do, and deal with Sade himself only indirectly. As was mentioned earlier, Kate Millet notes that death is frequent in male authors' treatment of women. Accordingly, Millet states that the best virtue that women can manifest is passivity, in order to survive male aggression.[22] Similarly, Germaine Greer says that women have become masochistic due to the stereotyped mode of behavior which has been imposed on them.[23] It is not completely fair to impute all of the crimes committed against women to Sade; nor can we expect to find an acceptable depiction of women in terms of post-1960 ideas and values. Sade was not the only man to have frequented prostitutes or to have abused them; his aristocratic condescension regarding women was not that exceptional. He did not invent pornography or bisexuality. But his literary inventories of possible abuses of women may never be equaled.

The most recent books which have appeared on Sade have been written by women. After the standard studies by Didier and Laborde (which have been referred to in the preceding pages), we have cited those of Gallop and Carter.[24] In all likelihood, women critics will continue to analyze and correct Sade for many years to come. In *Justine* and *Juliette,* we are not involved with the philosophical and political abstractions found in other writers of the eighteenth century (the best system of governments, religion and society, luxury), but more real situations involving human dignity and survival. While it is vastly different from other eighteenth-century French fiction, *Justine* remains the nucleus of Sade's literary production. The theme of persecution of virtue continues in his shorter writings of about the same period and into the historical novels written during the final years of Sade's life. While he varied his forms of expressing the assault on innocence, Sade was not able or willing to abandon the assault itself.

Chapter Four
Short Stories and Theater

Historiettes, Contes et Fabliaux

Sade wrote almost fifty short stories. Although they differ in form, tone, and message from his more notorious works of the same period, many of these tales borrow from and relate to the ideas and themes of *Justine* and *Juliette*.

The first major group of Sade's short stories is known as *Historiettes, Contes et Fabliaux (Short Stories, Tales, and Fables)*. These stories were written while Sade was in the Bastille in 1787 and 1788, and published for the first time by Maurice Heine in 1926.[1] The second major collection of short works, entitled *Les Crimes de l'amour (The Crimes of Love)*, was published in year 8 of the Republic (1800). The two groups were eventually differentiated by their author, but in several instances he announced his intention of combining them. In his *Catalogue raisonné* of October 1788, Sade indicated that he had written or at least outlined fifty *nouvelles*, including sixteen *historiettes*, thirty *contes*, a sequel to one of the completed tales, another *conte* transformed into a novel (probably *Les Infortunes de la vertu*), and two additional tales which were eventually deleted.[2] The *Catalogue raisonné* mentioned titles from both collections, as well as many of Sade's dramas. A similar tactic of blending the lighter stories from *Historiettes, Contes et Fabliaux* with the more somber *Crimes de l'amour* was announced in Sade's "Projet de refonte" of 1803–4.[3] Although Sade had already committed himself to a separate publication of *Les Crimes de l'amour*, he still clung to the principle of alternating the shorter, more humorous tales of the first collection with the sobriety and increased refinement of the second. The plan was thus: "These stories are mixed so that a gay adventure and sometimes even a smutty one, but still well within the confines of prudence and decency, is immediately followed by a serious or tragic adventure."[4] Whereas this pattern of contrasting tones was in fact abandoned, it reveals a new approach to fiction which was

60

not found in the predictable series of misfortunes and accumulation of cruelties of Sade's most infamous writings.

It will not be possible to account for all of the twenty-five units of *Historiettes, Contes et Fabliaux* in this study.[5] Some of them, for example, "La Saillie gasconne" ("The Gascon Witticism"), "Le Serpent" ("The Serpent"), and "Il y a place pour deux" ("Room for Two"), consist of a mere one or two pages and are so manifest in their tone and intent that they merit no further commentary. Others, such as "Le Président mystifié" ("The Mystified Magistrate"), "Emilie de Tourville," and "Augustine de Villebranche," are more extensive and intricate; they will be discussed in greater detail.

If some order is to be found in the twenty-five *Historiettes, Contes et Fabliaux,* it would have to be that of theme. Almost one half of these tales involve adultery: "L'Heureuse Feinte" ("The Fortunate Fake"), "La Prude" ("The Prudish Woman"), "La Marquise de Thélème",[6] "Le Talion" ("The Law of the Talion"), "Le Cocu de lui-même" ("The Self-made Cuckold"), "Il y a place pour deux," "L'Epoux corrigé" ("The Chastised Spouse"), "Le Mari prêtre" ("The Priest-Husband"), and "La Châtelaine de Longeville." Each of these centers on cuckoldry or marital infidelity. In "La Châtelaine de Longeville," for example, a double cuckoldry is depicted: Monsieur de Longeville is cheating on his wife, as she is on him. He arranges for her lover to be placed in a sack and drowned. But Mme. de Longeville learns of her husband's plan, and at the last moment she arranges for her husband's mistress to be substituted and drowned. The subtitle of this tale, "La Femme vengée" ("The Avenged Wife"), provides a short but comprehensive statement of content and message.

Several of the tales in *Historiettes, Contes et Fabliaux* relate sodomy to the motif of adultery. "Il y a place pour deux," "Attrapez-moi toujours de même" ("Take Me Always Thus"), "L'Epoux complaisant" ("The Obliging Husband"), "L'Instituteur philosophe" ("The Philosopher Teacher"), and "Soit fait ainsi qu'il est requis" ("Just as is Required") are those stories in which Sade continued to display a predilection for anal intercourse. Two of these are in fact so similar that the one is a virtual copy of the other. In both "L'Epoux complaisant" and "Soit fait ainsi qu'il est requis," a naive bride is warned just prior to the consummation of her marriage not to submit to her spouse's strange requests; she confuses the nature of the warning, refuses to make conventional love, and the husband is only too happy to oblige her otherwise.

Another set of tales from Sade's first collection illustrates the French cliché "Tel est pris qui croyait prendre" ("The Biter bitten, the Trickster tricked, the Tables turned"). They are "La Prude," "Le cocu de lui-même," "L'Epoux corrigé," and "Augustine de Villebranche." In each of these four instances, the machinations of the plotter are reversed and used against him, mischievously or maliciously. "Augustine de Villebranche, ou le Stratagème de l'amour" typifies this procedure, and at the same time is rather unique. Augustine, a beautiful young woman, has the reputation of being a man-hater, and prefers women instead. This inclination allows the narrator to give a brief but poignant defense of homosexuality not unlike Dolmancé's justification of the same practice in *La Philosophie dans le boudoir*. Augustine is then espied by Franville, and he plots to seduce her. Both attend a masquerade ball, she dressed as a man and Franville as a woman. Augustine invites the charming guest to a side chamber; after some caressing and partial disrobing, Augustine realizes that she has in fact attempted to seduce a man. Since she is not totally displeased by the new experience, she submits to Franville's long argument favoring heterosexuality, and marries him.

"Augustine de Villebranche" stands apart from Sade's typical portrayals of femininity, not only because of the heroine's initial sexual preference. Augustine is not the mindless victim exposed to the cruelties of men. It is she who leads the way in the comical seduction of Franville. In answering his question as to whether it is proper for women to have sexual inclinations toward other women, Augustine asserts her independence:

—Oh, it is different with us, it is restraint, prudence, even pride, if you wish, or perhaps even the fear of being handed over to a sex which seduces us for no other reason than to dominate us. But our senses still speak, and we console one another; when we succeed in keeping this hidden, an external appearance of discretion often results, and with that, nature is satisfied, decency is maintained, and morality is not offended. (14:165)

To evaluate this discourse in terms of its precedents in Sade's works, one would have to go back as far as *La Philosophie dans le boudoir,* and to Eugénie de Mistival. Similar to her, Augustine de Villebranche had the rare opportunity to obtain an education; in spite of her earlier inclinations, she chose to remain within the limits of commonly accepted behavior. Augustine's declaration stresses the abuse of women by men in positions of greater financial and political power. If women were to have any communications among themselves, they were forced to do so clandestinely. The consideration of equal justice toward women in Sade's work is, however, quite exceptional.

In contrast to this rare expression of independence for women, "Emilie de Tourville, ou la Cruauté fraternelle" ("Fraternal Cruelty") is more in conformity with the main lines of Sade's other fiction. Furthermore, it typifies the darker stories in *Historiettes, Contes et Fabliaux*. The tale begins *in medias res*, when the Comte de Luxeuil finds a girl injured and abandoned in a woods. He takes her to his home and has her cared for. The girl, Emilie, explains that when she once took a walk in the Tuileries gardens, as was her custom, she was rescued from a group of hoodlums by an unnamed young man; they fell in love and arranged for a series of secret meetings at the house of a woman named Berceil, until the latter tricked Emilie into changing the meetings to another site (14:137–43). With the new meeting house selected, Emilie was unfortunately caught by her two cruel and jealous brothers; they abused her, confined her to a remote country dungeon, and had her bled in order to debilitate her. The brothers also extorted a letter of rejection from her lover. But Emilie escaped and was rescued by Luxeuil. At the end of the flashback, Luxeuil arranged for the return and reconciliation of Emilie's lover, who happens to be his own son. He also succeeds in reuniting Emilie with her father, whose temperament caused Emilie's clandestine outings in the first place. Emilie's father agrees to marry his daughter to the young Luxeuil and condemns his cruel sons.

Aside from the surprise happy ending in the case of "Emilie de Tourville," the plot structures of *Historiettes, Contes et Fabliaux* are quite predictable. As opposed to the assertiveness of Augustine de Villebranche, Emilie is more similar to Justine: she submits, consents to anything and anyone, and never suspects or questions persons with overtly evil intentions. Her discovery by Luxeuil in the woods is a reminiscence of other Sadian heroines, notably Sophie in *Aline et Valcour* and Cécile in "Dorgeville." The identification of her lover as being her benefactor's son appears in a number of Sade's other tales, the most memorable instance of which occurs in "Florville et Courval" (see below). Finally, the message of "Emilie de

Tourville," that is, a scathing condemnation of hypocrisy (14:156), is present from the very subtitle of the tale, "La Cruauté fraternelle."

"Le Président mystifié" stands apart from the other component tales of *Historiettes, Contes et Fabliaux*. It is fully developed (the longest of the group), and contains several autobiographical references to Sade's experiences with judges. It is also the best demonstration of Sade's humor. In "Le Président mystifié," Mlle. de Téroze is forced by her father to marry the much older and ridiculous Fontanis, who is also the *président* of the Parlement d'Aix. She will be aided in her *mystification* of Fontanis by her sister and brother-in-law, M. and Mme. d'Olincourt, who are sympathetic to her love for d'Elbène. The forced marriage takes place. On the wedding night, Fontanis is given a potion which he believes to be an aphrodisiac, but which makes him ill and prevents him from consummating his marriage. The rest of the tale places more and greater obstacles in the path of the consummation: Mlle. de Téroze's friends continue to prescribe bogus remedies to Fontanis; when he insists that he sleep with his bride, he finds a hideous slave in his bed; he is forced to bathe in ice water, is glued to his bathroom seat, and is eventually forced to spend the night in a haunted castle. Fontanis is not undeserving of this harsh treatment; his amorous inclinations drive him to attempt the seduction of another girl, Lucile de Totteville, but he is caught by his wife and everyone else just at the moment of the attempted seduction. He finally agrees to sign a paper annulling the forced marriage, thus allowing Mlle. de Téroze to marry d'Elbène.

Together with the large quantity of slapstick humor (at one point, Fontanis is pushed into a pigsty) and a good amount of debauchery, Sade used his "Président mystifié" as a means of avenging some of the acts committed against him. The forced marriage of a young aristocrat (Mlle. de Téroze, in this case) to a magistrate of inferior social status might be Sade's expression of dissatisfaction at the marriage imposed on him by his father. Also, if we recall Sade's incident with the Marseilles prostitutes in 1772 and the fact that he was condemned to death and burned in effigy by the Parlement of Aix, we can appreciate more the following description of a *président:*

Very few people can imagine a judge of the Parlement of Aix, since he is a sort of animal frequently spoken of but never very well known, strict by nature, nitpicking, gullible, stubborn, vain, cowardly, rambling, and naturally stupid; as awkward as a gosling in appearance, with a stutter like Punch, and similarly lanky, long, skinny, and reeking like a cadaver. (14:172)

The past crimes of Judge Fontanis are enumerated, in particular one of 1772:

In 1772, a young distinguished man from this province wanted to innocently whip a courtesan who had played a bad turn on him, and this unfit lout turned it into a criminal case, calling it murder and poisoning; he ruined the young man, had him condemned to death *in absentia,* since he was unable to succeed in physically arresting him. (14:206)

In the end, the "mystified" judge, after being whipped himself, is counseled to show his bottom to the judges of Paris, since they took such keen interest in the case of Rose Keller's buttocks in 1768.[7]

The diversity of comic skills displayed by Sade in "Le Président mystifié" shows that the author was not a novice in the genre of short fiction. In his use of the farcical, the burlesque, and the bawdy, he demonstrated techniques which were used by earlier masters of the same genre. His indebtedness to Rabelais has already been mentioned. Since his short tales were intended for the public, as opposed to the clandestine, scroll-type works such as *Les 120 Journées de Sodome,* Sade endeavored to produce a refined, stylized literary product. His situation in 1788 was not unlike that of La Fontaine, who wrote one type of work, the *Fables,* for popular distribution, and another form, the *Contes,* from a lighter and more salacious point of view. The inventory of La Coste in 1767 listed works by other masters of short fiction, including Baculard d'Arnaud's *Contes et Nouvelles* and Marmontel's *Contes moraux* (1:269).[8] Sade had also read Cervantes, and, as we already know from the discussion of *Justine,* he was quite familiar with Voltaire. Perhaps because of his family origins and travels, he also delved into Italian literature, citing Dante and Tasso occasionally, and Petrarch. The Sade family genuinely believed that Laure de Sade was Petrarch's lover. As evidence of this belief, Sade quoted Petrarch's fifty-seventh sonnet in his "nouvelle italienne," "Laurence et Antonio" (*Les Crimes de l'amour,* 10:315–16), and even wrote a few lines in Italian.[9] If any one Italian author served as a model for Sade, it would have to be Boccaccio. Here we should recall that in his "Projet de refonte" of 1803–4, Sade arranged his more frivolous tales under the heading "Le Boccace français" (2:527–28). A general familiarity with the *Decameron* will reveal that Boccaccio did in fact treat themes common to Sade: adultery, lecherous monks and friars, bawdiness, and revenge.[10] But as is the case with Sade's potential borrowings from Voltaire and others, he adapted his material to suit his own special needs. The cruelty of Sade's darker tales and the emphasis on crime are not to be found in the *Decameron*. Although Sade was more relaxed in writing his *Historiettes, Contes et Fabliaux*, and although his means of attacking the persons responsible for his imprisonment are a moment of comic relief, he could not totally detach himself from the aggressive and sinister inclinations displayed in his other writings.

Concerning technique of the short story, we have ascertained two things: that the tales contained in *Historiettes, Contes et Fabliaux* vary considerably in length, tone, and plot, and that Sade's fundamental objective was to provide a series of contrasts between comic and tragic stories. In the discussion of *Les Infortunes de la vertu*, the problem of defining the novel (*le roman*) versus the short story or tale (*conte*) was posed. The same ambiguity concerning external form will occur in *Les Crimes de l'amour*. Various masters of shorter fiction have commented or even quipped on the issue. H. G. Wells defined the short story as "a piece of short fiction that could be read in half an hour." For Edgar Allan Poe, "in the whole composition, there should be no word written, of which the tendency, direct or indirect, is not one of pre-established design." John Hadfield emphasized the arbitrary nature of the problem in calling a short story a "story that is not long." And Chekhov cautioned the writer that if he described a gun hanging on the wall on page 1, sooner or later that gun must go off.[11] In French literature, allowing for precedents in the Renaissance and neoclassical periods, there appears to be common agreement that the short story reached its point of fruition only in the nineteenth century, with Mérimée, Balzac, Maupassant, and Anatole France as the major contributors.[12] In terms of criteria, the short story usually includes not only the basic elements of longer fiction (plot, theme, characterization, setting, point of view); according to one theory, it should also produce a single effect on the reader; it must have a feeling of immediacy; it must be judicious in the selection of its details, even if gaps or questions remain; and it must contain an element of suspense.[13] Without imposing these guidelines as rules on Sade, we can see that he was aware of most of them. His themes and messages are usually obvious and unfettered by other implications. What can we conclude from "Emilie de Tourville" other than that the cruel brothers deserved the chastisement which they received? In the shortest tales, for example, "L'Evêque embourbé" ("The Bishop Bogged Down"), only the bare minimum is stated to show that coachmen will indeed swear when their carriages become bogged down (14:105). "Le Président mystifié," more developed than the tales which precede and follow it, narrates dozens of pranks played on the judge from Aix, but the intricate relationships among the plotters and lovers are presented succinctly and economically. If Sade was deficient in any one aspect of the short story, it would be in the last category mentioned: suspense. Although not every short story has to be suspenseful, and although the principle of alternating humorous and tragic stories was a valid one, the tales which comprise *Historiettes, Contes et Fabliaux* become rather predictable. The outcome or conclusion of a tale of adultery or cuckoldry is never really in doubt in the mind of the reader, and the very pattern of contrasting moods tends toward repetition. Sade improved considerably in this regard with *Les Crimes de l'amour,* where he concentrated all of his creative strength on the theme which distinguished his most famous works, that of the persecution of virtue.

Les Crimes de l'amour

The twelve years which separated the *Historiettes, Contes et Fabliaux* from *Les Crimes de l'amour* showed marked improvement in Sade's abilities as a writer of short fiction. With few exceptions, the tales of this second collection regain the momentum acquired in the composition of *Justine* and *Juliette.* Although all of the *Crimes de l'amour* are written in prudent language, each story mirrors the old theme of virtue persecuted, and only two of them ("Juliette et Raunai" and "Laurence et Antonio") end on an optimistic or happy note.

Some of the themes present in *Historiettes, Contes et Fabliaux* can also be found in *Les Crimes de l'amour:* inconstancy in "La Double Epreuve" ("The Double Dilemma"), forced marriage in "Faxelange," and mystery in "Florville et Courval." Sade also resorts to the supernatural in "Rodrigue, ou la Tour enchantée" ("The Enchanted Tower"), and to incest, either implicit or explicit, in "Dorgeville," "Laurence et Antonio," and "La Comtesse de Sancerre." In his "Idée sur les romans," which was published as the preface to *Les Crimes de l'amour,*[14] Sade claimed to have a historical basis for two of the eleven tales, "Juliette et Raunai, ou la Conspiration d'Amboise" ("The Conspiracy of Amboise") and "Rodrigue." As was the procedure in his historical novels, however, the author merely acknowledges the historical point of departure, and proceeds in his explanation that the larger portions of the stories are pure invention. Consequently, we find an extremely magnanimous Duc de Guise at the end of "Juliette et Raunai" and the addition of a "multitude of events" to offset the "dryness" of the original version of "Rodrigue" (10:21).

If one of the eleven tales characterizes *Les Crimes de l'amour,* it would be "Dorgeville, ou les Torts de l'ambition" ("Ambition's Misdeeds"). Using the same introductory device found in "Emilie de Tourville," Sade has Dorgeville, a rich young bachelor, discover a woman, Cécile, who has just given birth to a child in a forest (10:380). Dorgeville takes her in, listens to her sad story of expulsion from her parents, and attempts to reconcile Cécile with the people whom he believes to be her parents (M. and Mme. Duperrier). The crisis occurs when, after marrying Cécile, Dorgeville learns that she and Saint-Surin, a trusted servant, are partners who conspired to rob and poison him. When the officials arrive to arrest the criminals, Cécile also reveals herself to be Dorgeville's lost sister. She kills her child just prior to being led off to prison; Dorgeville enters a monastery, where he dies two years later.

The main characteristic of Dorgeville is a limitless naiveté, which is sorely punished in the end, as is so frequently the case in Sade's opus. At no time does he question the tactics or the sincerity of Cécile and Saint-Surin. Since he relies on indirect evidence only, he could not have known that the prodigal daughter of M. and Mme. Duperrier was someone else. His feeble reaction to the startling revelation of the truth—the shedding of a few tears—conforms to the incapacity to think and act expressed by other Sadian heroes and heroines of similar natures.

The sudden and calamitous unmasking or recognition of villainy is more shocking in "Florville et Courval, ou le Fatalisme." The subtitle of this tale is an understatement, since it contains the most incredible series of coincidences and Oedipian relationships found in Sade's works. The outer story resembles that of "Dorgeville." M. de Courval wants to remarry, having had a mysterious and disappointing first marriage, and having fallen in love with Mlle. de Florville. In narrating her own story retrospectively, Florville tells Courval that, after being orphaned at birth, she was first sent to live with Mme. de Verquin, the wicked sister of her first benefactor. At Mme. de Verquin's home, she was seduced by Senneval, and became pregnant. Senneval left with the child, abandoning the mother. Florville then moved to the home of the virtuous Mme. de Lérince, and was courted by Saint-Ange. One night, Saint-Ange forced himself upon her; she stabbed him with a scissors. Although this act was adeptly concealed, Florville lived in constant fear of the sinister direction which her life had taken. She further witnessed the stabbing of one woman by another at an inn, and was forced to give testimony against the murderers. Upon completion of this inner story, Courval marries Florville, but their mutual bliss is, not surprisingly, of short duration. An incredible series of revelations unfolds when Courval's son returns. He informs his two listeners that he also knew a Mme. de Verquin; therefore, he was Senneval, Florville's first lover; he also learned that their son (Saint-Ange), had been stabbed by a woman trying to defend herself. Senneval then went to Nancy, where he found his mother (Courval's first wife), about to be executed because of Florville's testimony. Before her death, the condemned woman tells Senneval–Courval that she had had a daughter, whom she confided to a benefactor immediately after the birth. In summary, Florville is or was the sister of her first seducer, the murderess of her own son (Saint-Ange), the witness whose testimony caused the execution of Courval's first wife (and her mother), and both the daughter and bride of Courval. Upon learning her true identity, Florville shoots herself, and the two men (father and son) vanish into oblivion.

The adventure of "Florville et Courval" is an example of the Marquis de Sade at the height of his storytelling powers. If he had a weakness, it is one of excess in the complex system of *dévoilements* at the conclusion of the tale. The same desire for contrasts and oppositions expressed in his earlier works of short fiction is present in this unique story. The two women who sheltered Florville are direct opposites of one another: Mme. de Verquin professes a morality of *carpe diem* and condemns the monotony of leading a virtuous life (10:238), while Mme. de Lérince defends conventional religious practices at considerable length (10:224 ff.). Between these two parameters, Florville follows the horrible path of her destiny. In order to ease the shock of the eventual revelations and to enhance their plausibility, Sade includes a series of premonitory dreams. In the first of these, Florville relives the scene in which she stabbed Saint-Ange, and she foresees the cadaver of the woman (her mother), whom she was about to condemn through her testimony (10:236). And just before this dream becomes reality, the condemned woman admits to Florville that she had seen the latter in a dream of her own, which included visions of her son and of the scaffold (10:243). The nightmarish forebodings of these eventual realities are similar in technique to *Justine*. If we recall that Florville has just been married and that her misfortunes have supposedly come to an end, we can compare her uneasiness to that of Justine who was momentarily protected and sheltered after her long succession of abuses, but only to be struck down thereafter. As Béatrice Didier indicates, premonitions of death and disaster abound in preromantic literature, and compel the reader to follow the internal logic of the narration.[15] The tale of "Florville et Courval" provides us with the minimum information necessary to entertain these suspicions and, similar to the simultaneity involved with the epistolary novel, the premonitions are experienced at the same time that the characters live them. Although the quantity of recognitions presented at the end of "Florville et Courval" is implausible, the pace in which they are given is highly intense and effective.

Sade's best work of short fiction is "Eugénie de Franval," written in March 1788. He was fully aware of the superiority of this tale when, in his *Notes littéraires,* he called it "the purest and the most gay" of all the *Crimes de l'amour.*[16] "Eugénie de Franval" contains a number of common Sadian themes, and is one of the small number of his works which have been published in the prestigious Bibliothèque de la Pléiade.[17] It depicts a young rake, Franval, who marries Mlle. de Farneille and has a daughter, Eugénie. Thereafter, Franval assumes total control of this daughter's life, by imposing strict rules for her education, manners, and contacts with the external world. The purpose of all this severity is the eventual seduction of Eugénie, which is flagrantly realized (10:435). To placate the concerns of his wife and mother-in-law over Eugénie's well-being, Franval engages a friend, Valmont, to seduce Mme. de Franval. Valmont fails. Documents are forged so as to implicate an affair between Valmont and Mme. de Franval; this effort is not any more successful. When Mme. de Franval confronts her husband and daughter *in flagrante*

delicto, she implores her confessor, Clervil, to attempt to convince
Franval of his corruption and of the harm being done to their
daughter. Franval spurns Clervil and has him imprisoned. Franval's
ally Valmont turns against him, however, in the sense that he falls
in love with the irresistible Eugénie; the father allows him to view
her in the nude, but only in a carefully arranged setting in which,
by the use of ropes, Valmont can view any part of her that he wishes,
without being able to touch her. This elaborate scenario only serves
to increase Valmont's lust for the daughter. He kidnaps Eugénie,
is overtaken by Franval, and is shot by him. This act forces Franval
to flee abroad; with the promise to reform, he convinces his daughter
and wife to accompany him into exile, but in reality he plans to
murder his wife. In the end, when Franval must return momentarily
to France, he is robbed and beaten by highwaymen, and is found
wandering in the countryside by Clervil (who had begged his captors
to release him). Clervil informs Franval that his wife has just died
an agonizing death, which caused Eugénie to repent and to reform
her wicked life. Franval stabs himself.

As with *Justine,* Sade was quite aware that he had written an
extremely successful story with "Eugénie de Franval." And at this
point in our discussion of Sade's collected works, we can easily
recognize certain common motifs and situations. The young, idle
rake as depicted by Franval is a stock character in Sade's repertory,
as is the beautiful but neglected wife. It may be more than coincidental that Franval's parents had died at an early age and the son
was confided to a rich uncle for his education (10:426–27). The
violent degree of hatred against mothers and maternal roles has been
discussed at some length in preceding chapters; Franval is so bold
as to copulate with his daughter in the very presence of Mme. de
Franval. The stress placed on incest, the humiliation of religious
personages, and the degradation of innocent women are three other
motifs common to "Eugénie de Franval" and Sade's earlier writings.

Since the Marquis de Sade was actively involved in dramatic
writing and theatrical production at the time of his authorship of
Les Crimes de l'amour, he applied some of his techniques of drama
to his short stories. As will be treated in detail in the following
section, one of the tales in this group was directly transformed into
a drama. In "Eugénie de Franval," the scene in which Valmont
observes Eugénie is of special interest. If one recalls, Valmont asked
Franval to permit him the same voluptuous pleasures with the

daughter that the father had already experienced. Franval consents, but only to a point. To placate his friend, he constructs a pedestal for Eugénie, in the midst of an elaborately decorated room; she is to be dressed as a young savage leaning against a palm tree; the lighting arrangement accentuates her physical charms, and the "living statue" is separated by a canal six feet in width, to prevent Valmont from approaching her:

> At the edge of this configuration was placed Valmont's chair; a silken rope connected him to her; by manipulating this rope, he could make the pedestal turn so that the object of his worship could be perceived by him from all angles, and the positioning was such that, however she was moved, she was always extremely attractive. [Franval], hidden behind an artificial shrub, could simultaneously observe his mistress and his friend, and the viewing was to last one-half hour, according to the final agreement. (10:468–69)

When the allotted time expires, a gauze curtain descends, and Valmont must leave. This powerful scene was written by an author who had some sense of staging, machinery, and visual effects of the theater. Curiously, this libidinous scene was omitted from the original edition of *Les Crimes de l'amour*.[18] It has a wealth of possibilities for modern cinematographic adaptations, as do most of the principal scenes in "Eugénie de Franval." Akin to the other tales of the collection, its language is judicious, but without detracting from the erotic effect. Sade's commentary on the force and impact of this tale was as follows: " 'Eugénie de Franval,' one could call it, or the 'Evil Effects of Incest.' In all of European literature, there is no other tale or novel in which the dangers of libertinism are exposed with greater energy, nor any other somber work which is developed to a more frightening or pathetic level" (2:269). In short, the same spark of creative genius which was present in *Justine* reappeared in "Eugénie de Franval"; it is the showcase episode in *Les Crimes de l'amour*. Ironically, Sade could not separate himself from the impression made by his first masterpiece of 1791; the pamphleteer Villeterque attacked *Les Crimes de l'amour* in 1801, largely on the basis of the moral hypocrisy found in *Justine*.[19] Sade's scathing rebuttal, "L'Auteur des *Crimes de l'amour* à Villeterque, folliculaire," repeats the same principles set forth in his preface to *Justine* and in his "Idée sur les romans." If vice is to be avoided, it must be depicted in all of its horrible aspects. In "Florville et Courval," the horrendous list of fatal revelations is of the same nature as classical Greek legends. Crime was punished, according to Sade, at the conclusion of "Dorgeville," and in "Eugénie de Franval" the "monster who seduced his own daughter eventually stabbed himself" (10:512–13). Sade never found himself in contradiction with his claims of moral utility. He simply assumed the opposite point of view from conventional authors, and chose to punish virtue instead of vice. Although the approach was novel, it caused him considerable difficulties with the critics of his time and with later ones.

Theater

Sade's dramatic production testifies to the same diversity and profusion which are found in his short stories. His interest in the theater spanned his entire life. The manor at La Coste contained a theater where the author staged his earliest productions, and he had frequent amorous involvements with actresses. The *Catalogue raisonné* of 1788 lists more than two volumes of plays. Later, the economic situation in revolutionary France compelled the former aristocrat to earn his living from the theater. Thus in 1799, he accepted the position of *souffleur* ("prompter") at the Théâtre de Versailles. And as late as 1813, he continued to circulate manuscripts of his dramas to various theaters.

In 1970, Jean-Jacques Brochier published Sade's theatrical works in the Pauvert edition of Sade's complete works.[20] Brochier was assisted in his effort by Comte Xavier de Sade, who provided the manuscripts for "Tancrède," "Cléontine" and "L'Egarement de l'infortune" ("The Aberrations of Misfortune"), as well as personal letters and documents written by Sade. A precise chronological ordering of these dramas is almost impossible. Of the eighteen dramatic works printed by Brochier, thirteen were listed in the *Catalogue raisonné* as being in progress or completed. A few of them date from the years when Sade resided at La Coste; these include "L'Egarement de l'infortune," "Le Philosophe soi-disant" ("The So-called Philosopher"), and "Le Mariage du siècle" ("The Marriage of the Century"). A second group dates from the long period of imprisonment in Vincennes and the Bastille (1778–89): "Le Capricieux" ("The Capricious One"), "Sophie et Desfrancs," "Henriette et Saint-Clair," "Le Prévaricateur" ("The Corrupt Official"), and "Jeanne Laisné." Three of Sade's dramas were written and circulated during the revolutionary period: "Franchise et Trahison" ("Candor and Treachery"), *Oxtiern,* and "Le Boudoir." Three other works, "Les Antiquaires" ("The Antiquarians"), "L'Union des arts" ("Union of the Arts") (which includes five shorter plays), and "La Fête de l'amitié" ("The Celebration of Friendship"), probably date from Sade's final period of imprisonment which began in 1801. The four others, "La Tour enchantée" ("The Enchanted Tower"), "Les Jumelles" ("The Twins"), "Tancrède," and "Fanni," bear little or no chronological information.

Gilbert Lely, Sade's greatest admirer, dismissed his theatrical works as being of an "unbelievable mediocrity" (2:205). Both Lely's judgment and the works themselves deserve some further qualification. Sade's writing quality occasionally borders on the insipid and the unoriginal, as can be seen in "Le Philosophe soi-disant" and "Tancrède," but elsewhere he managed to produce some technical innovations, or at least successfully imitated the refinements of other dramatic authors. All of Sade's plays are written in judicious, prudent language. The notions of love, marriage, and morality presented in them are traditional, and most of the plays conclude happily. The theme of the persecution of virtue, which dominated *Les Crimes de l'amour,* is emphasized a number of times, in "Franchise et Trahison," *Oxtiern,* and "L'Egarement de l'infortune"; but the expulsion of the culprit or villain receives greater stress. An occasional suggestion of incest can be felt in "Sophie et Desfrancs" and "Henriette et Saint-Clair," but it is completely dispelled by startling recognitions of true identities at the conclusion of both plays. Otherwise stated, Sade struggled with the problem of originality within the narrow confines of the theater, but periodically allowed traces of his more libidinous tendencies to surface. In "Le Boudoir," for example, he borrowed a device from Molière's *Tartuffe* in placing Delcour behind a desk, so that he could eavesdrop on the conversation of his wife, whom he believes to be unfaithful. This play was rejected by the Comédie française, the Théâtre de la rue Feydeau and others, because the risqué dress of Delcour's wife and the casual manner in which the problem of adultery was treated were found to be unsuitable to contemporary moral standards (*Théâtre,* 2:90–91).

Since Sade intended at one point to introduce to the public his shorter fictional works in combination with his theater, the case of "Ernestine" and *Oxtiern* presents an appropriate example of the relationship between the two genres. "Ernestine," from *Les Crimes de l'amour*, was written during Sade's incarceration in the Bastille. *Oxtiern, ou les Dangers du libertinage*, was the dramatic adaptation of the short story, and the only one of Sade's plays which was fully produced. It was performed for the first time by the Théâtre Molière on 22 October 1791. The original tale is set in Sweden. Ernestine, daughter of Sanders, is in love with Herman, who struggles to make himself financially worthy of her love; but he depends on Mme. de Scholtz to achieve this independence, and since Mme. de Scholtz wants Herman for herself, she engages Oxtiern to seduce Ernestine. When Sanders, Ernestine's father, begins to delay in approving the marriage of his daughter to Herman, the latter tries to provoke Oxtiern into dueling him, but fails. Mme. de Scholz attempts to ruin Herman by removing the box of money entrusted to him. The cruelty of the two conspirators reaches its peak when Oxtiern forces Ernestine to view Herman's execution and simultaneously rapes her. Ernestine becomes aggressive after this atrocity and tries to avenge her honor by asking her cousin Sindersen to duel Oxtiern. The latter counters with a plan of his own: he arranges a substitution by which Sanders unknowingly stabs his own daughter, Ernestine. Oxtiern and Mme. de Scholtz are arrested. Sanders arranges for Oxtiern's release so that he may kill him honorably. And with a gesture of magnanimity worthy of Corneille, he spares Oxtiern, who leads an exemplary life thereafter.

In the dramatic adaptation entitled *Oxtiern,* Ernestine and Herman remain as characters. As the play begins, Ernestine (known here as the daughter of Falkenheim) has already been ravished and carried off by Oxtiern. They arrive at the home of Fabrice, where Oxtiern plans to exercise his philosophy that "the only way to win a woman's heart is by tormenting her" (*Théâtre,* 2:49). Since the drama is much more subdued than the tale, events transpire very quickly. Fabrice arranges Herman's release from prison just in time to prevent the duel between Ernestine and her father. The quid pro quo is then basically the same as in the tale, but the most ghoulish and perhaps the most imaginative element of the latter is omitted: since the assault on Ernestine had already occurred as the drama begins, the audience is not forced to witness it.

In 1791, Sade asked the Théâtre de la rue Feydeau to consider *Oxtiern.* The play was rejected with the explanation that the rescue by Fabrice of Herman was improbable; it was judged equally improbable that Ernestine could defend herself at all in a duel against a man; it was also mentioned that the author's style left a great deal to be desired (*Théâtre*, 2:11–12). Sade had clear ideas of what the classical French drama was intended to be; he displayed that knowledge in the polemics which accompany his dramas.[21] His problem of implausibility resulted from his effort to force an excessive amount of narrative material into the limits of the drama. As for the criticism of his style, many passages in *Oxtiern* are unnecessarily stilted, as seen in the following lament of Ernestine to Oxtiern:

Traitor, what alliance can you hope to arrange with me, when you have degraded me? Forever caught between opprobrium and humiliation, forever between chagrins and tears, tell me, Oxtiern, when you attempt to ensnare my beloved in the chains which he forged out of duty alone, what moments of calm and felicity could there possibly be for me on the face of the earth? Hatred and despair on the one hand, restriction and remorse on the other: the flames of our marriage would be enkindled only by the Furies; serpents would be our bonds, and death our only source of hope. (*Théâtre*, 2:56)

Ernestine's *préciosité* could be found suitable in other circumstances, were it not for the fact that she has already been ravished by the lecherous tormentor, and that in this scene her very life hangs in the balance. The dazzling rescues and expressions of magnanimity which conclude the drama would be more appropriate in a Cornelian melodrama than in the dire straits in which Sade places his personages.

Oxtiern was eventually received for production by the Théâtre Molière in October 1791, but its reception by the public was clouded by a *cabale* which occurred during the second performance on 4 November. During the second of three acts, a disconcerted spectator yelled to have the curtain lowered; it was brought down three quarters of the way, impeding the progress of the remaining scenes. Other spectators yelled to have the troublemaker evicted; some whistling ensued, but it was offset by the applause at the end (2:321–22). Through no fault of his own, therefore, Sade's only chance for a successful performance ended in failure.[22]

In defense of Sade's abilities as a dramatist, we should cite several examples of his use of established techniques and one or two instances of his innovations. A number of his plays ("Jeanne Laisné," "Les Jumelles," "Tancrède") were written in rather skillfully refined verse. He incorporated music into "La Tour enchantée," a comic opera blend of verse and prose, which was intended for inclusion in "L'Union des arts," but never performed. In "Sophie et Desfrancs," each of the first four acts is followed by pantomime scenes which serve as transitions in the complicated efforts of Mme. Armance to keep Sophie and Desfrancs apart. Since the practice of Greek choruses as transitions had long since been abandoned, Sade felt that his pantomimes would provide a logical substitute in his effort to present the "most perfect connections" in his dramatic action (*Théâtre*, 4:16). The principle of dramatic unity was put to a greater test in what amounts to a theatrical juggernaut, "L'Union des arts." This strange work was listed in the *Catalogue raisonné*, and seems to have been completed circa 1810. As its title implies, this colossal work purports to unite a great amount of material. According to the external intrigue, M. Desclapon, who is fond of the theater, intends to marry his daughter Emilie to his old and wealthy friend, M. de Vieuxblanc. But Emilie loves the Comte de Verceuil, and since the latter is very adept in theatrics, he stages five plays within the larger play in order to woo his beloved and to convince her father of his suitability. The intercalated performances are "Euphémie de Melun," "L'Homme dangereux" ("The Dangerous Man"), "Azélis," "Cléontine" and "La Tour enchantée."[23] Each of the inner plays serves the purpose of the larger framework: Emilie is publicly chastised for her coquettishness in "Azélis" (which is filled with magic, exotic beasts and complex machinery); in "L'Homme dangereux," the hypocrite Vieuxblanc is unmasked as the thief that he actually is, and so on. According to Sade, the idea for "L'Union des arts" was completely unique in its form (*Catalogue raisonné*, 2:263), and one must admit that the concept of the play as entrapment is put to effective use. But because of its complexity, "L'Union des arts" was never performed in its entirety, although "Azélis" was accepted by the Théâtre de Bondy and "L'Homme dangereux" (also known as "Le Suborneur") by the Théâtre italien (*Théâtre*, 3:104).

In view of Sade's original intent to combine the public presentation of his dramas with his shorter works of prose fiction, themes common to both genres become apparent: the forced marriage, the *Tel est pris qui croyait prendre* motif, and the punishment of the hypocrisy. The moderate language and judicious treatment of love found in the tales also typify his dramas; the extremism of his "secret" works is not to be found in either case. Strangely enough, Sade is known more today for a play about him than for any of those which he authored. The 1964 drama *Marat/Sade* has had a major role in determining Sade's image in the eyes of the modern public, for reasons which are both accurate and inaccurate.[24] As Peter Weiss admitted, his encounter between Marat and Sade in Charenton is totally fictitious, but the information given on Sade is based on a close acquaintance with the author's life and thought. Historically, Sade did produce dramas while in Charenton, and, as we have already mentioned, the official reaction to such activities was negative. The fact that Sade presented a funeral oration on behalf of Marat, the "Discours aux mânes de Marat" (11:117–22), provided further cause for Weiss to associate the two and to have them engage in a series of philosophical debates throughout his drama. In the Weiss play, Sade is positioned on a dais, like his "historiennes" in *Les 120 Journées de Sodome,* so that he can give stage indications to his players. He expounds on his philosophy of death as being a natural part of the life cycle, perhaps a reminiscence by Weiss of Dolmancé's creed in *La Philosophie dans le boudoir.* The Marquis de Sade also extolls the power of the imagination, and his self-styled portrait in the twentieth scene reveals the full extent of Weiss's blending of legend and fact:

> When I lay in the Bastille
> my ideas were already formed
> I sweated them out
> under the flows of my own whip
> out of hatred for myself
> and the limitations of my mind
> monstrous representations of a dying class
> who could exercise their power
> in spectacularly staged orgies . . .
> I dug the criminal out of myself
> so I could understand him and so understand
> the times we live in
> My imaginary giants committed
> desecrations and tortures
> I committed them myself
> and like them allowed myself to be bound and beaten[25]

This scene concludes with the flagellation of Sade by Charlotte Corday. The situation as presented in the 1964 dramatization is not unlike the chronicle of Sade's life prior to the long periods of imprisonment. A few incidents of notoriety created a legend which, when blended with an erotic and masochistic setting, was never significantly altered. The creation of monsters and decadent aristocrats while in prison permits the false generalization that Sade committed the atrocities of which he wrote. Thus madness and acts of cruelty continue to dominate the image of Sade in the twentieth century, just as they did in the latter decades of his life.

One cannot expect an author to excel in all of the literary genres accessible to him. In Sade's fifty short stories and to a lesser extent in his dramas, those which stand apart for their excellence and impact are the ones which borrow and pursue the themes and devices of the *Justine* sequence. When Oxtiern identifies himself as a "tormentor" of women (cf. above), he situates himself in an already long series of males whose sole function is aggression toward women. When the moment came for Sade to select historical figures for his novels of the 1807–13 period, he again chose women of superlative beauty who were subjected to the cruelties of vice and misfortune.

Chapter Five

Sade and the Eighteenth-Century French Novel

Aline et Valcour

The range of diversity in Sade's fiction is demonstrated further by his philosophical novel, *Aline et Valcour.* According to its author, it was "written in the Bastille one year before the Revolution of France."[1] More precisely, it was begun in November 1785 and completed in October 1788. As we know, this period was an extremely industrious one for Sade; the same years produced many of his short stories, *Justine,* and *Les 120 Journées de Sodome.* As one might expect, *Aline et Valcour* bears resemblances to these other works: the persecution of virtue, the abuse of a daughter by her libertine father, and different modes of behavior by two sisters.

After having identified this typicality and homogeneity, one must mention that *Aline et Valcour,* together with its interpolated stories, is unique among Sade's works. While it is true that the blending of philosophy and fiction spans all of his writings, and that these two aspects are the antipodes of eighteenth-century French literature, *Aline et Valcour* is more credible, more substantive than other Sadian productions. It is also more successful than his other novels from the technical point of view.

The fictional content of *Aline et Valcour* could be reduced to two questions: will Aline and Valcour be reunited, and who is the second daughter of Aline's mother, Mme. de Blamont? In the earliest letters, we learn that Aline's father, the président de Blamont, is opposed to the very idea of a wedding between Aline and Valcour. His opposition is ostensibly based on the fact that Valcour, of noble origins, is virtually penniless. Thus Valcour is forced to withdraw from the presence of the Blamont family's estate at Vertfeuille, but remains informed of activities there by letters from Aline, from her mother, and from his confidant Déterville. In the first of four intercalated stories, in letter 5 (15–27), Valcour relates to Aline his past adventures and experiences which, as explained in chapter 1, closely resemble those of Sade himself. In letter 15, Déterville comes upon a young distraught woman who has just given birth to a child in the forest near Vertfeuille. This discovery is a source of great joy for Mme. de Blamont, for she believes that Sophie, the unfortunate woman who explains in detail the horrors of her past life, is in fact her lost daughter; the misunderstanding is not fully clarified until letter 36. In the meantime, Blamont reveals through his own letters the scheme to hand his daughter Aline over to his fellow libertine Dolbourg. This stratagem is interrupted by the arrival at Vertfeuille of two mysterious wayfarers, Sainville and Léonore, each of whom narrates his or her past adventures in the longest interpolated stories of the work (see below). But these narrative detours have impact for the main plot, since Léonore will eventually be recognized as the missing daughter of Mme. de Blamont, and since we also discover that the président also plans to abduct Léonore. After the two lengthy philosophical digressions, events in the primary fiction unfold rather quickly. In letter 44, Blamont captures Sophie and eventually violates her. He attempts to permanently remove Valcour from the picture by bribing him, but to no avail (letter 46). He arranges for his men-at-arms to murder Aline's lover, but they fail also (letter 54). Blamont does succeed in eliminating his virtuous wife by poisoning her (letter 67), and immediately thereafter sequesters his daughter so as to force her to wed Dolbourg. But hours before the humiliating marriage, Aline stabs herself with a scissors, and thus preserves her chastity. According to the "editor" of the correspondence, Sainville and Léonore are at last free to live together in legitimate marriage and move to Vertfeuille, there to restore order and dignity to the family and its reputation. The lecherous Dolbourg reforms, but the corrupt Blamont flees and is eventually killed by bandits. Valcour dies in a monastery.

As can easily be seen from the recapitulation of these events, the central interest of *Aline et Valcour* remains the problem of evil.[2] The *jouissance de l'énonciation* or description of vice in minute detail, found in works contemporary to *Aline et Valcour*, is not to be found here. But vice remains in the forefront, as witnessed in the subterfuges of Blamont and Dolbourg. The old rhetorical claim of punishing vice by illustrating it is still present, however, in the "Avis de l'éditeur": "Ah! however prominent vice might be, it should never be feared except by its devotees, and if it should triumph, it will

only increase in horror in the eyes of virtue; nothing is more dangerous than to soften its attributes" (4:xxviii). Sade's self-praise
continues with the remark that authors such as Crébillon *fils* failed
to convince their readers of the dangers of libertinism, whereas he
has succeeded in his moral goal. If we compare the results of *Aline
et Valcour* to his other works written at the same period in the
Bastille, we may in this instance grant him the point.

We must also agree with Béatrice Didier in noting that *Aline et
Valcour* is Sade's most diverse creation.[3] When the interpolated
stories of Sainville and Léonore are added to the central fiction, the
resultant dimensions of *Aline et Valcour* are those of the picaresque
novel, the travelogue, and the *roman d'analyse*. Simone de Beauvoir
observed that the relationship between the Président de Blamont
and his wife closely parallels that of the author and Mme. de Sade.[4]
Together with the features of Valcour's self-portrait in letter 5, we
can also consider *Aline et Valcour* as being partially autobiographical.
This diversity of composition leads Didier to the further conclusion
that *Aline et Valcour* is a baroque novel which allows Sade to incorporate several different fictions into an ensemble.[5] In view of all
this complexity and the control of it, we must agree that it is one
of Sade's most refined literary pieces.

The letter or epistolary novel had been well established in France
prior to the appearance of *Aline et Valcour*. It was the narrative form
selected by Montesquieu and Crébillon *fils* in the first decades of
the eighteenth century. Rousseau and Richardson enhanced the popularity of letter fiction in the middle years of the century. The vogue
of novels written in letters continued until the end of the same
century, and then mysteriously disappeared and was replaced by
other narrative forms. Although the novelists of the Age of Enlightenment experimented with other narrative modes, epistolary
fiction was perhaps their most unique contribution to the novel.
One of the best accounts of the potentials and advantages of the
letter novel is found in Jean Rousset's *Forme et Signification*.[6] In
contrasting it with the third-person narrative approach, Rousset
explains that the epistolary novel allows the characters to narrate
their lives and adventures at virtually the same moment that they
live them; the reader participates in the immediacy and intimacy
of the experience. The novelist withdraws into the background and
assumes the role of editor, publisher, or he who "discovers" the
letters and who now makes them known to the public. Instead of

methodically describing and developing his characters, the writer allows them the freedom to sketch themselves. The result is a fragmentation of the narrative *optique,* and the presence of as many styles as there are characters. The multiplicity of points of views may also result in different accounts and varying interpretations of the same events—a process which Rousset identifies as the "chamber of mirrors" effect. Finally, when controlled with skill, the letter novel allows the device itself (the letter) to become an active agent in the fictional illusion: the placement and timing of a letter, or the omission of another, can create the impression that the correspondence is a genuine, unedited exchange of missives by the persons in question.

In the 1785–88 period, Sade was laboring with some extremely diverse and complex material. He was also in the process of acquiring formal skill and refinement as a writer. If the reader is disappointed by the predictable, cyclical pattern of events in *Justine* or the seemingly endless catalog of horrors in *Les 120 Journées de Sodome,* he must recognize the degree of artistic expertise realized in *Aline et Valcour.*[7] It has already been stated that the pretext for the letter exchange is the banishment of Valcour by Aline's father in the first pages of the novel. The style of the first letters from correspondents is direct and frank, as illustrated in Aline's earliest missive to Valcour: "My friend, we can no longer see one another. . . . There, I have said it, that cruel word; I was able to trace it without dying! . . . Imitate my courage. My father spoke to me as my master; he expects to be obeyed" (4:5). Although we do not find the mastery of individual styles used in *Les Liaisons dangereuses,* for example, we nonetheless witness differing tones and expressions utilized by the younger, persecuted lovers, versus the styles of the older, more secure characters. Sade further diversifies to the point of transcribing the primitive peasant dialect of Claudine, the wet nurse to whom the missing Blamont daughter was confided (letter 24).

In contrast with the more frequently adopted first-person and third-person narrative forms, the letter novel allows for more numerous insights and reactions to situations. Accordingly, two basic viewpoints can be identified in *Aline et Valcour:* that of the innocent but suspicious pair of lovers and that of the master plotters, Dolbourg and Blamont, originally known to the uninformed moral characters as "Delcour" and "Mirville." Whereas Aline is vexed by her father's rejection of Valcour but submits to his decision, Blamont's letters to Dolbourg provide an entirely different perspective, that of the supreme lechers, and reveal to the reader the scheme to corrupt Aline, Sophie, or Léonore. The rogues' situation is not entirely unprotected, however, since Dolbourg is unmasked in Déterville's first letter:

He bumped into [Aline] and actually arrived before us head first. The unexpected jolt, the sudden shaking of masses had slightly messed up his phony features; his tie flew in one direction, his wig in another, and the poor man, undone and uncapped, provoked such a spasmodic fit of laughter in my Eugénie that she had to be taken to the next room where I thought that she would faint. (4:3)

After this moment of comic relief, Dolbourg and Blamont turn their energies to more sinister plans. The presentation of their point of view allows Sade to capitalize on another feature of the letter novel, the multiple viewings and interpretations of the same event. In letter 44, Blamont triumphantly informs Dolbourg: "Sophie is ours," meaning that she has been successfully abducted to Blamont's castle. In letter 49, Sophie manages to send a letter to Mme. de Blamont, telling her that she has indeed been locked away and abused by her husband. The distressing effect of this news is temporarily suspended, since Valcour is attacked by Blamont's assassins in letter 54. In letter 57, Mme. de Blamont expresses her deep concerns to Valcour as to the whereabouts and safety of the kidnapped Sophie. The reader is in possession of the evidence of the crime as early as letter 49, but the characters are forced to wait until the various pieces of information are reconstructed before they can fully understand what we already know. Since Blamont still believes at this late point that Sophie is his daughter, he too has only partial information on the full reality of the situation.

As in all his other works, Sade's presence can be felt in *Aline et Valcour*. He does occupy the role of editor of the letters; but it is his own aesthetic principle which is communicated in these words of Déterville: "Unfortunately I have two libertines to depict; you must therefore be prepared for some obscene details, and forgive me for tracing them. I am not able to portray without vividness; when vice comes under my brush, I draw it with all of its tints, and so much the better if they cause shock" (letter 23). In the following paragraphs, we will receive more evidence of Sade's defense of portraying vice by the use of analogies with painting. Elsewhere in the letter novel, Sade addresses and dates his letters according to the needs and progression of his fiction; he editorializes quite frequently, explaining, for example, in Zamé's story a veiled reference to a notoriously cruel magistrate as being to Sartine, the dreaded lieutenant-general of police who turned a deaf ear to Sade's petitions for release after the Jeanne Testard scandal in 1763 (4:320–21). In other editorial interventions, he explains that some of the letters are either insignificant in themselves or repetitive of earlier ones, thereby justifying their deletion (for example, the note to letter 43).

From the point of view of structure, the Marquis de Sade makes good use of pairs of characters in *Aline et Valcour.* Each character relates to or is contrasted with another of similar age and status. The persecuted couple (Aline and Valcour) contrasts with the old and corrupt pair, Blamont and Dolbourg. Valcour confides in and corresponds with his trusted Déterville. The latter marries Eugénie (a friend of Aline), thus providing a working model of a happily united couple. Aline is associated with other women, initially with Sophie, believed to be her sister, and ultimately with Léonore, who is in fact her sibling. The most interesting pair of the series is perhaps that of Léonore and Clémentine: during the course of her forced travels in Europe and Africa, Léonore forever tries to remain pure and faithful to Sainville. Her traveling companion Clémentine suggests on numerous occasions that submission to male tormentors would be a more practical course of behavior than resistance. The differing approaches to the reality of various situations is definitely a reminiscence of a similar dichotomy in Sade's portraits of women, that of Justine and Juliette.

In his treatise on the novel and elsewhere, Sade expressed unlimited admiration for Jean-Jacques Rousseau. And Sade's epistolary novel can be considered as further homage to the author of the most popular French letter novel of the eighteenth century. The author's assumed role in *Aline et Valcour,* that of the distant editor who occasionally interrupts, is virtually identical to Rousseau's approach in *La Nouvelle Héloïse.* The emphasis on passion and the constant expressions of transported adoration of Aline by Valcour (for example, letter 3) are those of Saint-Preux writing to Julie. In letter 5, where Valcour reflects on his past life, we even find an imagined meeting between Valcour and Rousseau himself: "Rousseau was still living then; I went to see him; he had known my family; he welcomed me with that cordiality and frank civility which are inseparable companions of men of genius and superior talent; he praised and encouraged the plan that I had formed of renouncing everything in favor of studying letters and philosophy . . ." (4:25). Rousseau's "advice" to the young Valcour continues with the praise of life in the country, the condemnation of citadine society, and a eulogy of true virtue. After the unbridled lyricism, the exaltation of passion, and the literary form adopted, other fundamental tenets of Rousseauian philosophy will receive their praise in the travels of Sainville and Léonore.

L'Histoire de Sainville et de Léonore

The novel *Aline et Valcour* is interrupted by four *tiroirs* or interpolated stories: the shorter narratives of Valcour and Sophie, each containing a dozen or so pages, and two longer philosophical digressions. Sainville's story (including the narration of Zamé) occupies approximately 220 pages in the critical edition of Sade's works, as do the memoirs of Léonore. These longer insertions constitute letters 35 and 38 of the novel; in popular editions, they are printed separately. Although they do not appear to have direct bearing on the incidents of the complete work, they are the means used by Sade to combine the two major ingredients of eighteenth-century literature: prose fiction and philosophy. Similar to the other great writers of his time, Sade used the novel to illustrate *la morale en pratique*. His tendency toward cumbersome and unconnected adventures has been signaled in the treatments of *La Nouvelle Justine* and *Juliette*. It was to recur in *Adelaïde de Brunswick*. But the use of exotic adventure is justified in this instance.

The pretext for Sainville's narration was, if we recall, his arrival at Vertfeuille in search of refuge (letter 34). His marriage to Léonore was opposed by her parents; and when she is forced to enter a convent, Sainville arranges for her escape by having her pose as a statue of a saint which was to be carried off for repairs. In one of Sade's more humorous moments, an unsuspecting nun comes to pray to the statue on the eve of the planned escape, and when she attempts to embrace the statue on its face (Léonore had already turned in the opposite direction), the living statue could not keep herself from quivering. The fervent nun concludes that she has witnessed a miracle (4:165–66). The escape succeeds; Sainville and Léonore flee to Venice, but she is soon captured by pirates. The first step in Sainville's search for his lost mistress is in the kingdom of Butua (in Africa), where Sainville becomes the inspector of women slaves for Ben Mâacaro. It is there also that he is introduced to the philosophy of the exiled Portuguese, Sarmiento. After fleeing from Butua, Sainville arrives in Tamoé, ruled by the enlightened monarch Zamé, who also expounds on his system of values. Although Sainville is welcome to remain in the idyllic Tamoé, his love for Léonore pushes him on; he eventually rediscovers her in a theater in Bordeaux.

Adventure is subordinate to philosophy in the *Histoire de Sainville et de Léonore*. During his time spent with Sarmiento, Sainville assumes a role similar to that of Justine; he is a passive interlocutor during the Portuguese traveler's denunciation of the Franco-European system and his praise of the unconventional existence in Butua. Sarmiento instructs Sainville that what is called vice is not necessarily dangerous to men (4:202); that men are not born equal (4:205); that the English trade system in which everyone, including nobles, can exercise free trade is superior to the feudal and moribund French system (4:206); that climates are a determining factor in human behavior (4:208); that schools are pernicious to young people (4:224); and that in the general scheme of nature, man occupies an insignificant place (4:227). In place of the old world's values, Sarmiento praises the simplistic, albeit cruel, system of the Butuans with the additional observation that crime is nonexistent in Ben Mâacaro's kingdom (4:230–38). Unfortunately for Sarmiento, he is so attracted to this ruler's comfortable situation that he conspires to depose him, and is executed for treason (4:248).

It is evident that Sarmiento's observations conform to those of many eighteenth-century thinkers. Their prominent place in Sade's fiction corresponds to a long tradition of libertine spokesmen in his other works: Dolmancé in *La Philosophie dans le boudoir;* Bressac and others in the three versions of *Justine;* Saint-Fond and Noirceuil in *Juliette;* and eventually Brigandos in Léonore's story. The Sadian text always allows for extensive philosophizing on various aspects of the author's system of thought. Most of the works written in the Bastille were submitted to Mme. de Sade for her scrutiny, and in the case of *Aline et Valcour,* Sade's wife objected to Sarmiento's sophistries in defense of sodomy and theft, while she found merit in the subtle and delicate style used in the speeches of Sainville.[8] But Sarmiento is different from the libertine philosophers listed above; he merely reports the exotic and the unconventional, and does not possess the aggression and intensity of earlier Sadian representatives.

One of the unique aspects of *Aline et Valcour* is Sade's prediction of revolution in France. Since the novel was written in 1788 (the first printed edition appeared in 1795), we can appreciate the author's satisfaction in having foreseen the events which would entirely change the form of the French state. The prediction is echoed twice after the introduction, by Zamé (4:281) and by Brigandos in Léonore's recitation (5:140). Sade had an immediate motivation to call for the overthrow of a feudal regime into which he was born, but which at this time served instead to imprison him. In view of the date of publication of the novel, it was obviously to his advantage to vaunt the revolutionary government and to predict the arrival of it. Whereas the thrust of his philosophical writings is generally destructive, he at least made an effort to provide a workable alternative to France's legislative and judicial system. This alternative is the kingdom of Zamé in the latter part of Sainville's adventures. Zamé's state of Tamoé is Sade's version of utopia or Eldorado. In his life story as told to Sainville, Zamé explains how he became the benevolent monarch and freethinker that he is. He disallows parliaments and judges and their system of punishing men for obeying their natural impulses; he opposes convents and monasteries and favors pederasty. He criticizes Montesquieu particularly, because the latter's notion of political liberty is found to be unworkable (4:308). Instead of organized religion, the inhabitants of Tamoé worship a star in a most simplistic ritual. When Sainville inspects the other cities of the vicinity, he finds that all are similar to the one ruled by Zamé (4:343 ff.). Sainville's departure from Tamoé could not be more similar to Candide's exit from Eldorado. Zamé suggests that Sainville is a fool to relinquish the ideal life of his African kingdom, but Sainville is driven on in quest of his beloved Léonore. The large sums of money given to him by Zamé are as perishable as Candide's sheep laden with precious stones. The lesson derived from Voltaire's masterpiece, that men are not capable of preserving contentment when it is handed to them, is explicit in Sade's letter novel.[9]

Sade's *Aline et Valcour* is a compendium of other eighteenth-century common motifs. The travelogue aspect, which characterizes the *Histoire de Sainville et de Léonore,* began in the very first works of the century, notably Montesquieu's *Lettres persanes.* It continues in the works of Prévost, Voltaire, and Rousseau, and remains a dominant feature in Diderot's works near the end of the century (*Jacques le fataliste* and *Le Supplément au voyage de Bougainville*). In these travelogues and elsewhere, the themes of the relativity of beauty and morality dominate, and human diversity replaces the static images of the literature of the age of Louis XIV. Sade's philosophers, Sarmiento and Zamé, are thus permitted to criticize the old system and the dictated values of the *Ancien Régime*. The alliance of church and state also comes under attack here, as it does in varying degrees of radicalism in Sade's other works. Eighteenth-century literature added a new element to prior works: that of propaganda. Voltaire's *Candide*, Diderot's *La Religieuse,* and Rousseau's discourses, together with most of the other major works of the century, were written to persuade the public toward a cause or toward change. The great writers of the eighteenth century were critics more than revolutionaries. There is little, if anything, in the major texts of the Enlightenment which calls for violent revolt against the incumbent system. While some of the aspects of Sade's more extreme ideas remain in the philosophical digressions in *Aline et Valcour,* he fully integrates himself into the mainstream of eighteenth-century literature, by both the form and the content of this particular work, and thus lends further justification to its subtitle, "Le Roman philosophique."

The adventures of Léonore in letter 38 of *Aline et Valcour* merit a brief analysis. After her capture in Italy, she comes upon Dom Gaspard who guides her through the perilous regions of Africa, all the while revealing to her his philosophy of benevolent atheism. When Gaspard dies, Léonore takes on a new protectress, Clémentine, and miraculously survives a long series of assaults on her honor by pirates, cannibals, brigands, and inquisitors, together with a host of debauchees. Brigandos, the leader of a band of Gypsies, continues the long tradition of Sadian characters who earn their lives by crime and who profess the merits of robbery, incest, and libertinism (5:118 ff.). After recapitulating these persecutions, Léonore observes: "Alas, I had resources everywhere, but not a single one remained here [in the hands of a corrupt officer of the Inquisition], and I would either perish or God would have to work a miracle for me; and since the miracle of the Annunciation, I do not know of a single one that he has done in favor of women's virtue" (5:196). Miracles of a different order continue, however, just as the incredible persecutions continued in *Justine*. In contrast with her fictional sister, created at the same period, Léonore acquires some depth and individual identity. Sade was aware that he had written something special with *Justine*, as he indicated in his *Catalogue raisonné* of 1788; in the same text, he identified the originality of Léonore: "the most curious of these episodes is the one which follows . . . Léonore, separated from her lover Sainville, is attacked more than twenty times, and is placed more than twenty times in situations most critical for her virtue but without ever surrendering . . ." (2:266). This uniqueness is reinforced by several discourses made by Léonore at the conclusion of her narration. In the first of these, she criticizes the notion of charitable acts, a principle instilled in her by Brigandos and which shocks her mother, Mme. de Blamont (5:256). To defend herself, Léonore uses Marmontel's principles on sensations and pleasure and the relativity of definitions of vice and virtue, again to the consternation of Mme. de Blamont (5:256–60). Sade's Léonore is not an atheist but, as the editor of the letters cautions us, her expressed principles border on Deism. Her character is therefore different from the passive depictions of other Sadian women; she has a mind which she uses to form ideas based on her experiences, while her male counterpart (Sainville) clings to the standard values of expecting reward for charitable acts. In a penetrating analysis of this female character, Béatrice Fink states that Léonore, like Juliette and Eugénie de Mistival, is more developed and distinguishable than Sadian males, but she falls short of becoming an ideal woman:

Sade's utopian woman and her shortcomings may be redefined in terms of a non-Léonore. She is a nameless, faceless unit, not a personality with several names and an over-powering sexual appeal. She has never had access to the only life-instilling forms of education, those of varied experiences which strengthen individuality, of energy-generating struggles. Nor does she, like the thinking Léonore, reach a higher level of existence through the verbalization of her beliefs. And she hasn't the slightest trace of imagination. The non-Léonore lacks the requisite Sadian ingredients of success and power.[10]

Léonore's enlightened skepticism is more in conformity with the forensic superiority normally reserved for males. Having cited Fink's reservation, we must also add that Léonore's individuality is considerably greater than that of her sister Aline, and her expressed beliefs are very much in tune with predominant thought systems of the eighteenth century.

"Idée sur les romans"

The development of the eighteenth-century French novel witnessed a decline of the epic-historical and romance approaches, which dominated the majority of fictional works of the preceding century. The grandiose epic scale was supplanted by a movement toward individual, particular adventures, with the appearance of the best works of Prévost and Marivaux, ca. 1730. Personal memoirs, journals, and pseudo-autobiographies then became more and more concentrated on love stories, which characterize the French novel of the 1740–60 period, as typified by the works of Crébillon *fils* and Rousseau. Love stories are the essence of the French novel during this period, both as a cliché and in actual practice, but after Rousseau the novels written in eighteenth-century France followed a trend toward what is called *libertinage* and which is usually associated with the names of Laclos and Sade. Allowing for numerous exceptions in each, these trends dominated for a decade or two, and each movement seems to have suggested the nature and shape of the subsequent one.

Different from earlier, established forms of French literature, the novel was in a period of emergence in the eighteenth century. Daniel Mornet suggests that since there were no antecedents for it in classical literature, the embryonic status of the novel allowed it to develop freely and eventually flourish.[11] Most of the "theory" of the novel of this period has therefore been contributed in more recent times. Amid the wealth of this material, the 1963 study by Georges May, *Le Dilemme du roman au XVIIIe siècle,* is one of the most comprehensive and most reliable.[12] After citing the initial aesthetic inferiority of the novel, when compared to other established genres, May illustrates in detail its fluctuation between the "Scylla" of immorality and the "Charybdis" of implausibility, but notes that with the successes of Rousseau and others, the practice of prose fiction ultimately brought dignity to it. Another critic, Roger Laufer, compares the progress of the novel in eighteenth-century France to that of the cinema today, in the sense that it was the most frequently adopted and the most sought after form of artistic expression of its time.[13]

As was specified in the treatment of Sade's shorter works of fiction, the collection entitled *Les Crimes de l'amour* appeared in 1800 with an important prefatory essay, the "Idée sur les romans."[14] The date itself is significant, since Sade was in a position to make a comprehensive review of everything produced in France during the eighteenth century. Although it is partially a *pro domo* defense of some of his own writings, and a denial of authorship of others, Sade demonstrates in it a literary sensitivity unwitnessed previously, and many of his observations are superior to the ideas of his predecessors and contemporaries. In view of the vast scope of this document and its specific details on the novel, it seems more suitable to treat it here in conjunction with Sade's conventional novel rather than in the discussion of his short stories.

If we briefly pass in review the main prior judgments by novelists and critics on the novel, we become aware of a generally negative atmosphere. In his doctrinal statement on classical art in France, Boileau attached little importance to the novel; he dismissed it as being "frivolous" and "implausible" (*Art poétique,* chant 3, verses 119–21). Although Boileau's adverse judgment of 1674 had little impact on the writers who followed, a similar condemnation by Diderot was more harmful. In the latter's essay on the novel, *L'Eloge de Richardson,* he echoed Boileau in saying that prior to 1761 most French novels had been "a string of frivolous and imaginary events, the reading of which was dangerous for good taste and morals." He perceived artistic progress only in the English novel, and specifically Richardson's *Clarissa Harlowe, Pamela,* and *Sir Charles Grandison.* It was Jaucourt, not Diderot, who authored the entry "Roman" in the *Encyclopédie,* but this same denunciatory trend prevailed there also. The most perplexing instance of the contradictory situation of successful French novelists who condemned the very notion of their selected genre was that of Rousseau. True to his habit of using striking first sentences, he introduced his monumental *Nouvelle Héloïse* with the warning: "Theaters are necessary in large cities, and novels are needed by corrupt peoples."[15] Beyond Rousseau's flair for the paradox, this hostile theoretical attitude toward the novel, which commences in Montesquieu's editorial comments in *Les Lettres persanes,* continued in primary and secondary texts throughout the century. While theory and practice are characteristically separable, Sade was beyond this contradictory rhetorical battle; the evaluations of novels and novelists cited in his "Idée sur les romans" are valid to the extent that this work almost deserves an *explication de texte.*

Sade's admiration for Samuel Richardson was almost as deep as Diderot's, but it was put to a different purpose. Diderot emphasized the virtue and wisdom which could be derived from the example of *Clarissa;* but Sade claimed that Richardson and Fielding had taught the French that the old approach of always rewarding virtue was not the only one. From his acquaintance with later writers from England, Radcliffe and Lewis, Sade learned that greater intensity was required to dislodge the public from its usual complacency. The other major point from Sade's "Idée sur les romans," which has been discussed previously, was the demand for *élans* from novelists. This rule is not exclusive to Sade, but it does relate to a large portion of his own fictional productions, as do many of the other principles set forth in the document.

In the introduction to his essay on the novel, Sade poses three questions. Why does this type of work bear the title of novel? In what countries did the novel originate? And what rules must be followed to arrive at a degree of perfection in their composition? The use of the term *roman* is in itself curious. Other eighteenth-century novelists and critics were ambivalent in applying the term *roman* to the old romances and to that which we understand (in English) as "novel" today. As his remarks on seventeenth-century literature prove, Sade was most clear in distinguishing the two. According to him, the word itself evolved from *une romane,* as used in Romance tongues to refer to amorous adventures which we would consider romances. Although his proposed etymology is not totally accurate,[16] his approach is at least more scientific than that of his predecessors, who preferred to leave the concept in an ambiguous state.

In pursuit of his comprehensive analysis of the genre of prose fiction, Sade then traces the origins of the novel among the Greeks, Romans, Moors, and Spaniards. He cites the works of Heliodorus as being some of the earliest expressions of romance fiction (5:5), and most modern critics of the genre would agree with him. From Greece, the novel passed to the Moors, who then communicated it to the Spaniards and eventually to the French *troubadours.* Sade recognizes the superiority of Cervantes, claiming that he would be forever unequaled in prose fiction, and most people would again agree with the observation that *Don Quixote,* the first work which truly deserved the title of novel, may have been the greatest (10:9). True to his other convictions, Sade identifies a more immediate point of origin. Novels originated among god-worshipping people: "Man is subject to two weaknesses which ensue from his existence and which typify it. He must pray everywhere that he is, and he feels a need to love everywhere, and that is the basis of all novels" (10:5). The nature of these "weaknesses" is best illustrated in Sade's own writings.

As he draws nearer to modern times and to France, Sade mentions the contributions of the Gauls, Arthurian legends, and the *troubadours* in the gradual acquisition of a national literature. And consistent with his admiration of Italian literature expressed in other texts, he cites Dante, Boccaccio, Tasso, and Petrarch and notes that in the case of popular fiction it was France which influenced Italy, and not the opposite, which is generally true for Renaissance literature and the classical comedy. Concerning seventeenth-century French literature, Sade is equally perceptive; he identifies the two extremes of the novel of that century, the pastoral romance and the *roman d'analyse:*

To the degree that gallantry assumed a new appearance in France, the novel was perfected, and it was then, that is to say, at the beginning of the last century, that D'Urfé wrote his *Astrée,* which made us prefer, and rightly so, his charming shepherds of Lignon to the extravagant knights of the eleventh and twelfth centuries. . . . The astonishing success of *L'Astrée,* which was still read in the middle of this century, had completely captured peoples' minds, and it was imitated without being equaled. Gomberville, La Calprenède, Desmarets, Scudéry, all believed that they surpassed their original model, by substituting princes and kings for the shepherds of Lignon, and they fell into the trap which their model avoided. . . . After D'Urfé and his imitators, after the *Arianes,* the *Cléopâtres,* the *Polixandres,* in short, all those works where the hero, after languishing for nine volumes, was content to marry in the tenth one, after, I say, all of this rubbish which is unintelligible today, there came Mme. de Lafayette who, although tempted by the monotonous tone found in works which preceded her, shortened things considerably; and having become more concise, she became more interesting. (10:8–9)

This distinction between what could be seen as the ancient and the modern in French prose fiction is quite astute, especially when Sade's views are compared to those of his contemporaries. Today, we may have difficulty in understanding the popularity of the pastoral romances typified by D'Urfé's *Astrée,* but the seventeenth-century public, although limited in size, read them avidly. One admirer of *L'Astrée* was Rousseau; in his *Confessions,* book 4, he observed that it was this work which came back in his thoughts most frequently. Rousseau emphasized again the special place which *L'Astrée* held for him in 1767.[17]

In contrast with the generally insipid and lengthy romances of pre-Enlightenment fiction, Mme. de Lafayette's *Princesse de Clèves* is most frequently cited as the first truly modern French novel. Sade's mention of its brevity and resultant interest is accurate. *La Princesse de Clèves* is unencumbered; its development is gradual and psychologically profound; its structure closely resembles the unified framework of a classical tragedy, without the haphazard adventures of earlier romances.

In a brief overview of other women novelists, Sade ascribes limited praise to Lussan, Tencin, Graffigny, and Riccoboni, among others (10:10). It appears that he was not totally at ease with the idea that women could assume the career of writing. After a paragraph of mixed praise of Fénelon, Sade commences his evaluation of eighteenth-century novels. He begins by identifying an important shift away from earlier fiction:

The writers who appeared thereafter felt that trivialities would no longer amuse a century perverted by the Regency, a century which had recovered from the follies of chivalry, religious extravagances, and the worship of women; they found that it was easier to amuse or to corrupt these women, instead of serving or adoring them; thus they created events, scenes, and conversations more in conformity with popular taste. (10:10–11)

If the eighteenth-century novelists had achieved a break with the romance tradition, they were not totally free from another error, according to Sade. The first major novelist of that century reviewed by Sade is Crébillon *fils,* and he notes that the author of *Le Sopha, Tanzaï,* and *Les Egarements du coeur et de l'esprit* flattered vice at the expense of virtue. There were in fact two facets of Crébillon: he who wrote mildly pornographic tales as a satire of his society, and the more refined author who contributed *Les Egarements du coeur et de l'esprit.* Sade obviously maintains himself aloof from such criticism.

Marivaux is the next author to come under Sade's scrutiny. Sade finds him to be more original than Crébillon but with one reservation: "But how, with so much energy, could anyone have a style so precious and mannered? He proved that nature never gives a novelist all of the gifts necessary to perfect his art" (10:11). Indeed, the most complete study of Marivaux to date, that of Frédéric Deloffre, analyzes the author of *Le Paysan parvenu* and *La Vie de Marianne* from the point of view of his "préciosité nouvelle."[18]

Sade's greatest praise is, naturally, reserved for Voltaire and Rousseau. As we know, Sade possessed complete sets of the works of both authors. For him, *Candide* and *Zadig* would always remain "pure masterpieces" (10:11), and Rousseau's *Nouvelle Héloïse* "will never be equaled" (10:11). References to Voltaire in *Justine* and *Aline et Valcour* merely augment this superlative admiration. His distinction of the radically differing approaches used by these two giants of eighteenth-century French fiction is also astute: "While Momus was dictating *Candide* to Voltaire, love traced with its torch all of the burning pages of *Julie*" (10:11). When we recall that seventy-two editions of Rousseau's novel were printed between 1762 and 1800, and more than fifty different editions of *Candide* appeared between 1758 and the French Revolution, we realize that Sade's recognition of their superiority was in tune with contemporary and modern preferences.[19]

After a brief mention of Marmontel and after two pages of superlative praise of Richardson and Fielding, Sade confers distinction on l'abbé Prévost who wrote the French equivalent of *Moll Flanders* (*Manon Lescaut*). Prévost is an aggregate of all that which Sade admired in the novel. He was believed to be the translator of the first French edition of Richardson's novels;[20] from among his dozens of pseudohistorical novels, only *Manon Lescaut, Clèveland,* and *L'Histoire d'une Grecque moderne* stand apart as true masterpieces (the same three titles are mentioned by Sade). Given his sentimental effusions and exoticism, Prévost is frequently compared to Rousseau as a precursor of romanticism. In the negative column, Rétif de la Bretonne (designated with an initial only in the text) is accused by Sade of inundating the public with his "terrible productions" written in a low and rampant style (10:14). This hostility is exceptionally intense in "L'Idée sur les romans"; it is explained by the fact that Rétif, not unlike Sade in some regards during the 1790–1800 period, had attacked Sade's works in *Le Pied de Fanchette, Monsieur Nicolas,* and *L'Anti-Justine.*[21]

There are three salient omissions in Sade's review of eighteenth-century novelists: Montesquieu, Diderot, and Laclos. Although he remained silent on *Les Lettres persanes,* he criticizes Montesquieu's idea of political liberty in *L'Histoire de Sainville et de Léonore.* We know that Sade was familiar with Diderot's works, as stated in the prior discussion of his philosophic sources. The strangest omission from the list of novelists is that of Pierre Ambroise Choderlos de Laclos, whose *Liaisons dangereuses* of 1782 was, after Sade's works, the most significant contribution to the French novel between 1762 and 1800. Sade knew of Laclos and his *Liaisons dangereuses;* it was listed in the inventory of his books while in the Bastille. Since these two authors are very frequently grouped together in anthologies and general studies of the French novel, Sade's silence on Laclos is perplexing. We also know that both writers were imprisoned in the Picpus asylum from 26 March until 15 October 1794.[22] Gilbert Lely offers two hypotheses for this curious silence: either Sade was jealous of Laclos's success with *Les Liaisons dangereuses,* one which he had not fully realized himself; or, in view of their simultaneous presence in Picpus, these two "infamous" novelists may have indeed met and argued. Given Sade's violent temperament, both theories seem quite plausible.

Further evidence of the Sade–Laclos similarity and direct evidence of influence by the latter on the former are found in two precious pages of Sade's *Notes littéraires* of the 1803–14 period. They contain a "Plan d'un roman en lettres" (15:29–30). The "plan" calls for a young and innocent girl named Clémence, whose situation closely resembles that of Laclos's Cécile in *Les Liaisons dangereuses.* Clémence confides in and is ruined by an aunt and tutor, Théodorine, who possesses "a great deal of wit and wickedness" (a perfect Marquise de Merteuil). Théodorine is to be assisted in her scheme by Delville, age thirty-five; it is he who seduces Clémence, as Valmont did to Cécile. Clémence is to have an unnamed lover who, like Danceny, is seduced by Théodorine. The conformity of Sade's plot to that of *Les Liaisons dangereuses* is so close that it is regrettable for literary history that Sade did not complete his projected imitation.

Most people would agree that Sade's completed epistolary novel, *Aline et Valcour,* was a success from the technical point of view. In general, its letters are logically arranged and pertinent to developments in the plot. But it would come as no surprise to have Sade "lose" in any comparison of his epistolary skills with those of Laclos. He simply paid less attention to the finer points of variation of styles of the correspondents and strategic placement of his letters. Some of his past narrative habits, for example, the long philosophical insertions, took precedence over the refined use of letters. Laclos was more judicious: he typifies the observation of Mallarmé, who said: "To name a thing is to eliminate three fourths of the delight of a poem, which is the joy of guessing little by little; but to merely suggest it, that is the ideal." Mallarmé's criticism of the Parnassian poets applies equally well to Laclos's moral principles, in that he too wrote of sex and seduction, but avoided explicitly graphic scenes.[23] In spite of his tacit dismissal of Laclos, Sade did not escape the nearly incessant association of his work with that of Laclos. A contemporary review in the *Tribunal d'Apollon* discerned a slight amount of difference between the two, albeit an unflattering one: "It has been proved that it [*Les Liaisons dangereuses*] has done more harm to morality in the last few years than all of the productions of this type have done in an entire century. The infamous novel *Justine* is the only one which can compete with it for criminal superiority in the number of victims in it."[24]

With the identification of a new emphasis in the novel as derived from the works of Mrs. Radcliffe and "Monk" Lewis, Sade's review of the novel is complete. In the closing pages of "L'Idée sur les romans," he provides answers to the third question which he had posed: what are the rules governing the genre? Since the novel was an emerging genre, rules received little attention from previous writers and critics of the century. It is only in a few prefaces and personal writings that we find serious discussions of the art of fiction.[25] One might consider strange the provision of rules for the novel by the Marquis de Sade, when his practice was most unconstrained. But the Sade of 1800 was vastly more subdued and mature than the author of the Bastille manuscripts.

After the vociferous insistence on *élans* and the requirement that novelists use the full array of the colors of hell (10:14), Sade turns to a more conventional aspect of the novel: moral utility. To the question of the practical use of novels, the response is quite blunt: "What do they serve indeed, hypocritical and perverse men, for you alone ask this ridiculous question; they serve to portray you just as you are" (10:15). Horace's precept of *utile et dulce* can be found in almost every introduction to eighteenth-century French novels; if the road leading to moral edification was occasionally paved with bawdiness, the principle at least remained intact in every novel from Montesquieu to Sade. The latter's emphasis on moral profit was tempered, however, with a comment added several pages later, when he recommends that writers avoid the affectation of moralizing completely (10:18). Sade's approach to morality is unique, as we have seen in prior discussions of his major and minor works; he was faced with a contradiction which he never fully solved. More practicable rules for novelists of the future are a knowledge of the human heart, which Sade considered as the most important (10:16); together with that knowledge, the writer must be natural, since he is the child of nature (10:16); finally, Sade forbids his disciples to stray from verisimilitude (10:16). These last three recommendations are facets of the doctrine of a refined writer. As he proved in *Aline et Valcour* and in other regular texts, he was capable of gaining from the wisdom and prudence of neoclassical aesthetics.

On the subject of technique, Sade is equally frank. The writers who preceded him had very little to say about the finer points of their craft. "L'Idée sur les romans," on the contrary, makes suggestions regarding correct style, the need to establish an outline, how to maintain the reader's interest, the fact that subplots should derive from and relate back to the main one, and the denouement should be of a logical and gradual order (10:17−18). Disregarding Sade's practice, we must at least admit that these criteria were written by a conscientious author who was sensitive to the more complex issues of the novel. They increase in value when one recalls that few other French novelists wrote at such length and detail on the art of the novel.

The last four pages of "L'Idée sur les romans" are the polemic portion of the essay. Keeping in mind that this treatise was introduced as a preface to *Les Crimes de l'amour,* Sade cautions that the stories contained therein do not totally respect his general rules. In the same spirit of candor, Sade explains the extent of his borrowings for two of the tales, "La Tour enchantée" and "La Conspiration d'Amboise." In his final paragraph, he defends the intensity of his portrayal in *Aline et Valcour,* while denying authorship of *Justine.* The rhetoric used is typical of Sade: "Never, I say it again, never will I paint crime other than wrapped in the colors of hell; I want it to be completely exposed, then feared, and finally hated, and I know of no other way to do this except to show it in all of the horror that accompanies it. Woe unto those who shroud it with roses" (10:22). It is fitting that Sade's most important aesthetic pronouncement be concluded with references to *Aline et Valcour* and *Justine,* since they are the antipodes of his literary productions. For Sade to defend his intensity of portraying vice with the example of

Aline et Valcour is an easy victory, since this work is most discreet. The reference to *Justine* in a text written in 1800 shows, however, that this work had not gained acceptance with his public. Sade was then and remained the author of the "infamous" *Justine*. His theoretical treatment of the novel is dignified without reservation. While his vantage point was only slightly better than that of Rousseau, Diderot and others, his insights and evaluations are less prejudiced and more perspicacious. Sade's situation is not unlike that of Boileau; while the novel was emerging in the eighteenth century, the best theoretical accounts of it came afterward (those of May, Showalter, Mornet, Brooks, Coulet, Rousset, Stewart, Sgard, and others).[26] Finally, when Sade adds at the end of his treatise, "And we also know how to create," he occupies a place which he has earned in the hierarchy of Enlightenment prose fiction.

Chapter Six

Historical Novels

History and Fiction

Sade's historical novels form a curious triptych which stands independently at the end of his career. Since he viewed himself foremost as a *homme de lettres* and since these three works are quite typical of his age, they are worthy of some attention. The three quasi-historical novels are virtual contemporaries. *La Marquise de Gange* was written during the 1807–12 period, and published in 1813; *Adélaïde de Brunswick* was written in 1812; *L'Histoire secrète d'Isabelle de Bavière* was completed in 1813. The last two novels were not published until the twentieth century. [1]

In spite of vast differences of tone and orientation among these three works and the author's more notorious publications, their composition is not that incongruous with earlier tendencies. Some of Sade's *contes* ("Jeanne Laisné," "Juliette et Raunai") were centered around historical incidents. The *Juliette* saga contained a series of references to the papacy and to the dynasties of various Italian cities. We also know that the prisoner of the Vincennes dungeon in 1783 planned an "Eloge de François Ier." [2] And when we recall that Sade's uncle wrote a life of Petrarch and that the Sade family believed that Laure de Sade was the lover of the Italian poet, we can better understand the point of view of the chronicler in *La Marquise de Gange* who refers to himself as a "descendant of Laure" and who wrote four short verses in praise of her charms (11:321). Finally, the prisoner of the Charenton asylum, in addition to composing and directing plays for the inmates during the years 1807–12, was in full possession of his creative abilities, and disposed of a great deal of time to elaborate on the lives of three known historical figures.

In all three instances, the Marquis de Sade commenced with an existing historical document of either a famous personage (Isabelle and La Marquise de Gange) or a lesser known one (Adélaïde of Brunswick), and magnified his source into a somber tale of persecution. In the case of La Marquise de Gange, he dared to publish the document which accounted for her tribulations, an episode in *Faits des causes célèbres.*[3] In *Adelaïde de Brunswick* however, the author simply referred to a "historical fact of the eleventh century" in his final note, and gave no further clarification of his sources. Although his three historical novels technically belong to the nineteenth century, their reshaping and amplification conform to a long-standing tradition of the eighteenth century. The distinction between history in the sense of accurate chronicle and history as story was clear in Sade's mind, even though the French word *histoire* was at the time used ambivalently.[4] We have seen that in his "Idée sur les romans," Sade identified two English novelists, Richardson and Fielding, as being superior in their genre. Henry Fielding exploited the ambiguity of the terms involved by referring to *Tom Jones* and *Joseph Andrews* as "histories." But Sade cautioned that the duties of the historian were to "reveal man such as he is," whereas the role of the novelist was to "show man as he could be, or as he is revealed by the changes of vice and the throes of passion" (10:12). The most flagrant instance of a novelist who openly blended fiction and history was l'abbé Prévost, another writer cited for distinction in the "Idée sur les romans." Prévost's more famous works, *L'Histoire du Chevalier des Grieux et de Manon Lescaut* and *L'Histoire d'une Grecque moderne,* were passed off as authentic memoirs. In more obvious cases such as *L'Histoire de Guillaume le conquérant* and *L'Histoire de Marguérite d'Anjou, reine d'Angleterre,* the departure from a historical basis to enter the realm of fiction is more evident. The eighteenth-century public was not duped by such pseudohistorical allusions any more than we are today. In this regard, Sade's method is comparable to that of Defoe, Stendhal, and more recent authors, for example, James Michener and Antonia Fraser, who select an entire historical epoch, a family, or an individual, and trace them through generations. They are free to give references or to omit them, to "quote" people as they supposedly spoke, without indicating where fact stops and where fiction begins. Sade's final contributions to literature conform to this pattern; they are written discreetly, like his shorter tales and *Aline et Valcour;* they also continue the theme of the persecution of innocence and virtue, in medieval and modern frameworks.

La Marquise de Gange

The setting for Sade's first historical novel is the reign of Louis XIV and the incidents of what we would consider today as a famous

murder trial of a beautiful woman by her two brothers-in-law.
Euphrasie de Rossan is wed first to the Comte de Castellane, who
dies shortly after the marriage. She is of remarkable beauty, and
known as "la belle Provençale." She is said to have caught the eye
of Louis XIV himself and Queen Christina of Sweden, although
Sade does not elaborate on these claimed infatuations. Her second
husband, the Marquis de Gange, transports her from Paris to his
estate near Montpellier. There, after a short period of happiness,
mingled nonetheless with premonitions of evil to come (nightmares,
storms, black coffins), Euphrasie has the misfortune of being lusted
after and pursued by her two brothers-in-law, the lecherous abbé
Théodore de Gange and the less ingenious but equally corrupt Chevalier de Gange. The first major conspiracy by l'abbé to wrest Euphrasie away from her husband is indicative of the rest of the narration:
forced to spend a night in the castle of Tarascon, the abbé assigns
rooms and keys to his brother, Euphrasie, the Comte de Villefranche
(a co-conspirator), and Ambroisine, a courtesan, so that the Marquise
surprises her husband in the arms of the latter. Distraught, Euphrasie flees with Villefranche; they are overtaken by bandits; Euphrasie is returned to her husband, and Villefranche is killed by
him. After a brief allusion to his historical source (the fact the
Euphrasie is due to inherit a large sum from her mother, and which
all three brothers want for their own family), and after a bit of
history concerning Avignon, Sade continues with the assault on
Euphrasie's virtue, all the while claiming prudence and fidelity to
his sources (11:324). Since Euphrasie is blackmailed by l'abbé with
incriminating notes written under duress and since he is unable to
force her to succumb to him, his wrath is unleashed. In the narration
of the final tortures and death of Euphrasie, Sade claims that he
transcribed word for word his written source. According to that
account, a weak poison fails to kill Euphrasie; thus her irate assassins
(l'abbé and the Chevalier) force her to choose her form of death: the
sword, pistol, or another poison. She takes the latter, asks for a
moment alone to make her confession, attempts to flee and to vomit
the fatal liquid, and seeks refuge in a nearby house. Her aggressors
pursue and discover her; the Chevalier crushes a glass in her face,
then stabs her twice in the chest, and five more times in the back.
Unbelievably still alive, Euphrasie begs for protection from her
husband Alphonse, but he is interested only in her repudiation of
the will which would prevent her inheritance from passing to the
Gange family. Euphrasie dies nineteen days after the first attempts

at murder; the Marquis is stripped of his titles and banished; the Chevalier and l'abbé are condemned to death on the rack, but both escape. The Chevalier dies in battle as a mercenary; l'abbé de Gange flees to Holland, marries, and, according to *Faits des causes célèbres,* survives unpunished.

In conformity to his claimed role of didactic, Sade adds several paragraphs to the document, in which l'abbé de Gange is shot by a mysterious intruder six months after his marriage. This modification is peculiar, because it runs counter to the main thrust of his work wherein vice is usually rewarded and virtue humiliated. The addition could be excused by Sade's oblique remark in his preface, "Everything was not explained in the memoirs," but that remains highly unlikely. A more probable reason for the punishment of l'abbé de Gange is introduced with a new statement of purpose: "the desire to please virtuous people" (11:188).

La Marquise de Gange is a short work which reads quickly and which maintains the reader's interest throughout. The only exception to this unity of narration is the series of digressions by l'abbé Théodore de Gange. But as is frequently the case in neoclassical literature, verbal aggression is as significant as physical attack, and Théodore's long monologues are an important weapon in his arsenal. His philosophical discourses are also the primary means by which Sade transformed his rather short documentary of the life of "la belle Provençale" into a novel. One must also acknowledge that Théodore is the character of central interest. From the earliest of Sade's writings (the *Dialogue entre un prêtre et un moribond* and *Les 120 Journées de Sodome*), and throughout the following ones, corrupt priests have been omnipresent. In *La Marquise de Gange,* Théodore is not the only one of his kind; the local vicar, l'abbé Perret, cooperates in Théodore's schemes to seduce his brother's wife. But in contrast with the supreme criminals of earlier works by Sade, Théodore never succeeds in his plot. Dungeons, abductions, and murder are inadequate to win Euphrasie. In a penetrating analysis of Sade, Pierre Klossowski notes that the Sadian hero lives in the realm of exasperation, and we must admit that Théodore is exasperation incarnate.[5] He can also be viewed as an expression of Sade's overactive libido, protesting against his failed conquests, frustrations, and desires.

The depth of psychological analysis of Théodore is not to be found in the other characters of *La Marquise de Gange.* Sade never mentions nor justifies why, after two conspiracies by her brothers-in-law, Euphrasie submits to a third one, when she allows Théodore to lead her into a darkened room, expecting to find her husband there, but is instead forced into the embrace of a young stranger, and then surprised by her husband. Nor is it explained why the husband himself does not suspect his brothers of malfeasance. We know that he is interested in his wife's money, but his actual feelings toward her remain vague. Finally, the third brother (the Chevalier) appears to be no more than a pawn in the service of his lecherous brother. It appears as if Sade contented himself with an implicit statement of a case of incest, without expanding it to the degree found in "Eugénie de Franval," for example, or in *Juliette.*

In the process of transforming a short historical account of the life of the Marquise de Gange into a novel, Sade required a considerable amount of additional material. He remained faithful to his original source only in the narration of the heroine's death. After the philosophical digressions, the embellishments and additions in question were the repeated and unsuccessful attacks on Euphrasie, which never existed in the *Causes célèbres,* and which constitute the novel. In his preface, Sade prepared his reader for the acceptance of these additions:

> May the people who wish to acquire precise information in the history of the woeful Marquise de Gange read us with the interest inspired by truth; and may those who prefer to find a bit of fiction, even in purely historical narrations, not accuse us of having utilized anything but a story which contains truth in every line and pure and simple facts, since the reading of it would be unbearable without the accessories with which we have surrounded it; and when one realizes that the subject treated will of necessity be shocking, it is certainly permissible to surround it by all that can prepare one's soul to accept it without too much cruel distress. (11:188)

The aim was therefore to appease both types of clientele, those who preferred history and those interested only in fiction. But the effort at accommodating both groups was bound to entail difficulties for Sade. The "accessories" to the original account were severely criticized in Michaud's *Biographie universelle:* "With the intention of making his heroine more interesting, the author has only debased her by having her succumb to the most vulgar pitfalls."[6] This evaluation of Sade's novel was assuredly prejudiced by the generally negative attitude found in all of Michaud's entries concerning Sade.

As will be explained in greater detail in the discussion of *Adelaïde de Brunswick,* elements of gothic fiction are more prominent in Sade's historical novels than in any prior works. Accordingly, on the eve of Théodore's arrival, Euphrasie has a series of dreams which forewarn her of the evils about to happen (11:200 ff.). Later, she is compelled to visit the tomb of her husband's family, where she will eventually be laid to rest (11:264). The visit is enveloped in mist, distant church bells, and is terminated by the mournful sounds emanating from the tomb. After being kidnapped and taken in the direction of Cadenet (a small village in the Vaucluse), Euphrasie seeks a moment of rest in a gloomy castle, only to find a partially dissected cadaver in the first room which she enters (11:337); her shock at this sight is immediately followed by cosmic disturbances and a violent storm. These are merely a few of the other "accessories" included by the author in the endless persecution of his innocent heroine.

If additions and embellishments were a major factor in Sade's transformation of the legend of "la belle Provençale" into a novel, several omissions are equally interesting. The first is the infatuation of King Louis XIV with Mme. de Gange, which is historically valid, but mentioned by Sade only in passing in the first pages of his novel. The author must have considered himself too near to this source to develop it, and thus felt prevented from digressing on a well-known and quite recent era. The other omission concerns a similar fascination for the Marquise de Gange by Queen Christina of Sweden, daughter of Gustavus Adolphus. According to Vincent Cronin, Christina, who had the reputation of being a transvestite, espied the Marquise on a visit to France:

At Lyons, Christina surprised the lovely Marquise de Gange bathing in the Rhône. "What a masterpiece of nature!" she cried, kissing the Marquise on the throat, the eyes and the brow. Unable to persuade her to share the royal bed, she wrote the Marquise a long love letter: "While waiting for a pleasant metamorphosis to change my sex, I want to see and adore you, tell you every moment that I adore you."[7]

The exclusion of such a provocative and erotic encounter by Sade is perplexing. In his earlier writings, he would have developed such an incident to the fullest detail. And as will become evident in the treatment of Isabelle de Bavière, the author did not hesitate to associate extreme perversion with known historical figures. But even *Isabelle de Bavière* is vastly more subdued than Sade's works written prior to 1800.

L'Histoire secrète d'Isabelle de Bavière

Amid the dismal atmosphere of the Hundred Years' War, the struggles for power among the dukes of France, and the ineptitude of Charles VI, Sade weaves the tapestry of "crimes" of Isabelle of Bavaria, whom he also refers to as "la grande gore" (15:340), a *marâtre* ("unnatural mother") and whom he epitaphs as "une louve" or she-wolf (15:389). According to his version, Isabelle begins to form political and amorous alliances immediately after her marriage to Charles at the age of sixteen. Her first lovers are Bois-Bourdon and Craon, and she arranges for the latter to kill the Connétable de Clisson, in her quest for power. Among her more unique stratagems in Sade's interpretation of her life are the proposal of a new crusade, supposedly to free the Holy Land, but only to rid herself of Charles (15:288–89), and a *danse macabre,* also known as the "bal ardent," where Charles narrowly escapes a gruesome death. As he promised, Sade gives us the impression that Isabelle was responsible for every major political assassination committed between 1385 and 1420 in France. She thus prostitutes herself first to Bois-Bourdon, then to each of the rival dukes, Burgundy and Orleans, until the death of the latter becomes a political necessity (15:357). Her penchant for vice and violence involves large numbers on occasion (for example, the Armagnac and Cabochien revolts) and is even directed against her own children, with the alleged murder by poisoning of three of them, and numerous efforts to assassinate Prince Charles. Isabelle welcomes the succession of her son-in-law Henry V to the throne of England, so that she may present him with almost total control of France, by terms of the Treaty of Troyes. After the victories of Charles VII and Joan of Arc, and after realizing that her days are numbered, since all of her cronies have abandoned her, Isabelle dies an ignominious death, but not without arranging for the execution of Joan.

A few qualifications of the charges by Sade against Isabelle must be made. The liaison with her *grand maître d'hôtel,* Louis de Bois-Bourdon, seems to have been accurate, according to Michaud and other biographers. But the second allegation of a love pact with the

duke of Touraine (15:277) is exaggerated preparation for the more
serious accusations which follow. Historically, Isabelle made little
effort to conceal her affair with Louis, duke of Orleans, her brother-
in-law, but the charge of a ménage à quatre involving Charles,
Isabelle, and the duke and duchess of Orleans (15:291) is equally
exaggerated. Sade claims that Isabelle was able to induce Charles's
periods of mental instability with drugs; other historians claim that
she treated him with extreme kindness during these crises. Sade's
Isabelle provokes the Marquis de Craon into killing Clisson, but I
have found no substantiation of this charge. The "bal ardent" episode
was, according to Sade, engineered by Isabelle with the intent of
burning Charles to death, while she would look on indifferently
(15:309). According to Barbara Tuchman, the scheme was arranged
by Huguet de Gursay.[8] Four of the six men who were dressed as
wood savages in wax, pitch, and hemp rags did in fact die; but
Charles was saved by the duchess of Berry, who had the presence
of mind to smother Charles's flames with her dress; no other mention
is made of Isabelle's guilt or intrigue. Sade purports that the Dau-
phin Prince Charles was the son of Isabelle and the duke of Orleans,
not Charles (15:335–36). There has long been speculation as to the
legitimacy of Charles, most of which seems untenable. The Isabelle
in Sade's novel actively seeks the death of Joan of Arc; if we were
to add the thesis that Joan was herself the daughter of Isabelle and
Orleans, the result would be the ludicrous situation of Charles VII
and Joan having been brother and sister. Sade claims that Isabelle,
together with Jean *sans peur,* duke of Burgundy, conspired to murder
the duke of Orleans in 1419 (15:357). According to Bainville, only
Burgundy was guilty, because he suspected Orleans of having seduced his wife.[9] Finally, Sade gives the impression of total responsibility by Isabelle for the disgraceful Treaty of Troyes. Michelet,
for one, judges Isabelle less harshly.[10] She did in fact sign the treaty,
as did the duke of Burgundy; and she was interested in having her
daughter Catherine marry Henry of England; but she simply did
not have the political support to have arranged the entire situation
herself.

Of the three novels written at the end of his career, Sade's *Histoire
secrète d'Isabelle de Bavière* is the most historical, based on the magnitude of the personages and the era selected, the abundance of dates
and details, and the structuring of the work into three chronolog-
ically distinct parts, all of which permit us to read it as history

more than as fiction. Similar to the approach used in *La Marquise de Gange* and *Adelaïde de Brunswick,* Sade omits graphic and erotic descriptions and details. Nonetheless, he endeavors to inventory all of the crimes imputed to Isabelle, as if he were writing a medieval version of *Les 120 Journées de Sodome.* His intent is manifest in his preface: "the truth is that one can reasonably prove that not one drop of blood was shed during this terrible reign which was not shed by her; that not a single crime was committed for which she was either the cause or the object" (15:254). We do not therefore find a total reduction or relaxation of the force and intensity of Sade in his portrayal of vice in 1812. The implications of debauchery, adultery, and incest are as present in *Isabelle de Bavière* as they were in his more infamous works, but are neatly veiled in a quasi-historical setting.

In his introduction and throughout the text of *Isabelle de Bavière,* Sade claims to have had access to new sources unavailable to other historians. They were the interrogation of her lover Bois-Bourdon and the last will and testament of the duke of Burgundy. He claims to have viewed these papers in the Bibliothèque des Chartreux in Dijon in 1764 and 1765; indeed, the chronicle of his events and travels at this period corroborate a visit to Dijon. On 26 June 1764, he formally addressed the Parlement of Burgundy, accepting the commission of lieutenant-general of Bresse and Bugey. In May of 1765, en route with Mlle. de Beauvoisin from Paris to Avignon, he passed through Dijon again.[11] But when Sade was asked by prospective publishers to deliver these documents, he claimed that they had been burned during the Revolution (see the appendix entitled "Note sur plusieurs des pièces justificatives énoncées dans cet ouvrage," 15:491). Among the historians who analyzed Isabelle's behavior and whom Sade criticizes for their conservatism are l'abbé de Choisy, Mlle. de Lussan, Le Laboureur, Méserai, Enguerrand de Monstrelet, and Villaret. As was mentioned earlier, however, none of these historians nor those of more recent years are as critical of Isabelle.[12] When Sade asks that we not accuse him of attempting to multiply the horrors and atrocities of which he accuses her (15:370), he immediately continues the list of horrors, thus revealing a rather profound fascination with the degree of corruption attained by her.

In preceding chapters, Sade's misconception of women in general has been explained; most of his heroines are victims (the Justine model) or merely objects to the end of male gratification. Adelaïde de Brunswick and Euphrasie de Gange are also brutally victimized; we will soon see how the portraits of these last two women fit the predictable pattern of female innocence and abuse. In contrast, the mode of behavior found in *Juliette* indicates the counterpart of passive victimization: Juliette was turned loose in the world to wreak the havoc previously reserved for Sadian males. Isabelle stands apart from these generally stereotyped patterns; or, viewed from a different angle, her promiscuity is the political application of the Juliette form of behavior. The subordination of her personal feelings to interests of state could not be more Machiavellian (15:275). At one point, she dressed in commoner's clothing so that she could frolic in the dens of thieves and murderers (15:424). Surrounded by weak male figures (Charles VI, her son, and lovers), Isabelle's lust for dominance and tyranny remain unchecked. When Sade pauses to describe Isabelle, we are able to see and understand these two aspects of uniqueness and the narrator's fascination for her:

With the graces and charms customary for her age, there reigned nonetheless in the traits of Isabelle a degree of pride which was uncommon at the age of sixteen. In her eyes, quite large and very dark, one could read more pride than the sensitivity which is so sweet and attractive in the innocent looks of a young woman. Her figure was indicative of prestige and litheness; her gestures were distinct, her gait was fearless, her voice a bit harsh, her speech succinct. Much haughtiness in her bearing, no trace of that tender humaneness, the appanage of noble souls which, as they draw near the throne, consoles them for that painful distance in which fortune has them born. Already demonstrating an indifference for morals and religion which might bolster her; an insurmontable aversion for anything which contraried her tastes; inflexibility in her dispositions; excess in her pleasures; a dangerous inclination toward vengeance; easily finding fault in all that surrounded her. . . . At the same time avaricious and prodigal, wanting everything, invading everything; ignorant of the price of anything; holding herself alone in value, sacrificing all interests, even those of the state, to her own ends; contented with the rank where destiny placed her, not for the purpose of doing good, but instead to find impunity amid evil; possessing all the vices, finally, which were not redeemed by a single virtue. (15:272).

In this exceptionally detailed description of Isabelle, we find elements of both the *portrait physique* and the *portrait moral*. But the aspects of the former are soon abandoned in favor of those of the latter. Those qualities which are so unique in Isabelle are the pride and vice which gradually rise in importance in the middle section of the portrait, to the point that the person in question has to be considered as a serious threat to the rest of humankind. If we have difficulty in conceiving how a young woman would already be so corrupt and threatening, it is because Sade had considerable difficulty in creating realistic portraits of women. In his philosophical works, his short stories, and his last works, his female characters are best described by their actions or by those of others. The author leaves us no room for doubt as to his desired interpretation of his heroine. In dozens of instances, he directly addresses his reader in calling for the condemnation of Isabelle's corruption. Outbursts such as "Having seen Isabelle conduct herself in all matters with so much deceit and hypocrisy, how can one be surprised by what she will subsequently accomplish?" are not uncommon.

If Sade had been interested in painting an accurate historical portrait of Isabelle, he would not have gone to such length to condemn her before the evidence against her could have been weighed. Furthermore, a recent historian's depiction of Isabelle is quite different from that of Sade. According to E. A. Lucie-Smith, Isabelle had a marked physical defect (shortness of one leg) which was passed on to her son Charles VII. She was ostentatiously pious also, which conflicts with the Sade version of her:

the Isabelle of the period was a much degenerated being, both morally and physically. Physically, she had become grotesquely fat. By the end of 1409, she had already reached a point where it was considered doubtful, because of her obesity, whether she could any longer act as regent of the kingdom, should the need arise. She also became gouty, and in 1415 had to have a wheelchair made in order to get about.[13]

The same commentator observes that Isabelle was acutely phobic, having a great fear of such things as thunder, disease, and bridges. Considering the physical problems from which she appears to have suffered, and her phobias, one might indeed question the accuracy of Sade's violent portrayal of her.

One possible explanation for the extremism used in Sade's presentation of the woman who reigned in France from 1385 till 1435 might be of a personal nature. Since Sade was aging and his own physical health was deteriorating, he was still searching for a means to end his imprisonment. By his unremitting condemnation of Isabelle, he seems to have assumed the role of defender of his country, in order that the disasters of Isabelle's reign might be averted by the incumbent one. This assumed role becomes apparent in passages such as the following: "Oh woeful country! Allow us to shed our tears for a moment over the misdeeds which tore you apart during this despicable alliance! The rivers of blood which she extracted from you have reddened your breast for so long that when we deplore the evils of those horrible days, we also lament those of the last century" (15:354). The comparison of the decadence of the late medieval court of Charles and Isabelle with that of the French court on the eve of the Revolution is repeated elsewhere in the novel:

> Louis [Orleans] was ignorant of the place that this young nobleman [Bois-Bourdon] occupied in the queen's heart; but we know that Isabelle did not conceal from Bois-Bourdon the fact that her brother-in-law was her lover; therefore he became the confidant of his mistress but without having the same intimate relationship with his rival. Such peculiarities can be found only at the most corrupt of royal courts; those of the eighteenth century could provide us with a few more examples. (15:281)

Sade's historical parallels are astute and perhaps personally motivated. If we recall that the Sade family had arranged with the Bonaparte regime for the transfer of the aging Marquis from Sainte-Pélagie to Bicêtre in 1803, then to Charenton in the same year, and that as late as 17 June 1809 Sade was still petitioning the emperor for his release,[14] we might view *Isabelle de Bavière* as an effort to diminish the past misdeeds of the author of *La Nouvelle Justine* and *Juliette;* the extremely patriotic criticism of a past disgrace would then have been written for use by the current government. If such was Sade's intent, it failed, since Napoleon twice ordered (in 1811 and 1812) that the Marquis de Sade remain in confinement.[15]

Adelaïde de Brunswick

In his manifesto of the novel written in 1800, Sade criticized the *romans précieux* of D'Urfé, La Calprenède, and Mlle. de Scudéry for all of their "unintelligible rubbish" (10:9), and welcomed the advent of Mme. de La Fayette, who put an end to the old and exaggerated romances. If excessive adventure was seen as the main weakness in these earlier works, it recurs as a problem in Sade's third historical novel, *Adelaïde de Brunswick*. As in the case of the two other ones,

Adelaïde de Brunswick includes elements of history, gothic literature, and aspects of Sadian fiction, but does not have the charismatic attraction of the character of Euphrasie de Gange, nor the historical significance of the reign of Isabelle and Charles VI.

The primary setting for *Adelaïde de Brunswick* is eleventh-century Saxony. Its ruler, Frederick, arranges to marry Adelaïde of Brunswick by proxy, with the trusted Louis of Thuringia serving as his representative. After a brief mention of Frederick's problems in maintaining autonomy against the military pressures of Emperor Henry IV, and after a passing reference to Henry's dispute with the pope (Gregory VI) and the problem of investiture, Sade commences a long series of macabre adventures which serve to keep Frederick apart from his bride. Adelaïde soon reveals that her true affections are for Louis, her symbolic husband, and she indiscreetly confides this to Mersbourg, who also loves her and who conspires to separate her from the two other men in her life. Since Mersbourg possesses the secrets of Frederick's heart also, he has Adelaïde arrested and imprisoned while she is supposedly on her way to a rendezvous with Kaunitz; the latter is summarily executed for treason. Adelaïde flees to Mersbourg's castle with Major Kreutzer and his daughter Bathilde, who will remain at her side for the duration of her adventures. Frederick leaves Louis in control of Saxony and sets forth in search of Adelaïde, and the dual approach begins. The scene changes back to Adelaïde, who has just been captured by Schinders, brother of the unjustly executed Kaunitz; Schinders forces Adelaïde and Bathilde to weave the very rope with which he will hang them. But a grotesque hunchback (Stolbach) aids them to escape, disguised in male clothing; the effort fails, and they are recaptured. Meanwhile, Frederick and Mersbourg are led to the house of a magician who, with a crystal ball, shows them the whereabouts of Adelaïde. Later, Adelaïde and Bathilde are rescued from their captors by Frederick and Mersbourg, but neither pair recognizes the other. Frederick, returning home to save Saxony from the emperor, is arrested by Henry's troops, but Mersbourg is able to make his way back to Saxony. At this point, Adelaïde is in Frankfurt and is courted by the Margrave of Baden. She and Bathilde are soon kidnapped by Dourlach, one of Baden's "gentlemen," and are quickly liberated by a gang of bandits led by Krimpser, who was indebted to Adelaïde's father. The hapless princess of Brunswick is led to Padua, then to Venice, where she becomes embroiled in a political conspiracy. Back in Saxony, Louis has had time to rescue Frederick; the latter and Mersbourg set out again in search of Adelaïde. Their search is partially successful in Venice, where Frederick catches a glimpse of her at the Venice carnival, but she flees him. Adelaïde and Bathilde arrive at a secluded convent, where the nuns spend their time preparing their own graves. Finally, Adelaïde is reunited with Louis and Frederick and triumphantly returns to Dresden. Tranquillity is of short duration, however. Mersbourg reveals the Adelaïde–Louis affair to Frederick, who insists on a jousting match to avenge his honor. Louis wins, Frederick dies, and according to local protocol, Adelaïde must marry Louis. Yet she cannot agree to wed her husband's victor and withdraws to the remote convent mentioned above, where she takes vows and dies soon thereafter, but not before Mersbourg confesses that it was he who organized most of the abductions and misdeeds which led to the final calamity.

In *La Marquise de Gange,* Sade contented himself with the expansion of a short, concise case; in *Isabelle de Bavière,* he judged abundantly. In *Adelaïde de Brunswick,* he becomes lost in a maze of disconnected adventures. Gone is the emphasis on gore, lechery, and crime, and the condemnation of them. The historical basis for *Adelaïde de Brunswick* is hastily acknowledged and then dismissed in a short note at the conclusion of the work:

A historical item from the eleventh century occasioned that which has just been read, but the author, having found in Adelaïde merely one more of those odious characters which our manners cannot tolerate, was compelled to make rather considerable modifications and amplifications, so that to him alone must one attribute almost all of the merits of the creation. (15:245)

The "historical item" in question, left without further specification, probably revealed to Sade that Adelaïde (ca. 1030–1100) married Frederick, prince of Saxony, and conspired with her lover, Louis, Landgrave of Thuringia, against her husband, and married Louis in 1059.[16] Adelaïde, Frederick, and Louis are historically authentic, but the characters of Mersbourg, Kaunitz, and the remaining secondary figures are examples of the "considerable modifications and amplifications" for which the author assumed responsibility. Adelaïde is obviously the worthy successor of la Marquise de Gange, and is equally naive and unsuspecting. She is inconstant, proclaiming her love for Louis on the one hand, and seeking the comfort and glory of the crown of Saxony on the other. Her inconsistency becomes apparent in Venice, where she momentarily entertains the affections of Contarino (15:190–91). Her reaction to the hideous Stolbach's demand of money as the price of her freedom is somewhat absurd: "Oh Stolbach, you are a fine fellow, yelled Adelaïde. At least you will cause anguish to no one by this action. The sum which you require at this moment is perhaps a bit excessive in view of our present means; but one way or another, we will give you all that you require" (15:135). Whether we are to view Adelaïde as a passive damsel in distress or as a feudal Justine at the mercy of her captors, the fact remains that her prosaic responses and inconsistency of behavior leave her without depth or plausibility. Her character development remains plastic and rigid—another cold portrait in the gallery of Sadian women. Instead of depth and plausibility, we have presented to us hunchbacks, morbid nuns, and a vast array of bandits.

If characterization was a problem for Sade, his effort at the dual approach of maintaining two simultaneous points of view was also unsuccessful. If we recall that the incidents occurring to Adelaïde and those happening to Frederick are presented at the same time, we find that these two perspectives are shifted with little or no transition by the author, and with no other justification than an occasional "Meanwhile" or "Let us now return to. . . ."[17] Also, the propagandizing and moralizing which distinguished *Isabelle de Bavière* is missing in *Adelaïde de Brunswick*. In their place are found several digressions: one on the abuse of justice (15:140–45) and another on the city of Venice (15:180–81). But these narrative detours do not have the compelling urgency or philosophical significance of the digressions in *Les 120 Journées de Sodome* or *Juliette*.

Adelaïde de Brunswick is the most gothic of Sade's three historical novels and of his entire works. We have already mentioned that the best known works of Matthew Lewis and Ann Radcliffe appeared too late to have had any great impact on the *Justine* and *Juliette* series. Sade's view of these gothic writers from England became clear in 1800, when he praised them in his preface to *Les Crimes de l'amour*. It was to them that he attributed an important change in the perspective of the novel:

For those people who know all of the sufferings which evildoers may cause
other men, the novel was becoming as difficult to compose as it was
monotonous to read; there was not a single person who could not have
experienced more misfortunes in four or five years, than the most famous
novelist in literature could have depicted in a century. It thus became
necessary, when composing works of interest, to call hell itself into the
picture, and to find in imaginary worlds that with which people were
commonly familiar. . . . (15:15)

The invocation of hell is the point at which the Marquis de Sade
ceases to belong to the eighteenth century and joins the ranks of
the following one. The abandoned monasteries, constant danger
from evildoers, and the suspense found in the English novelists of
the 1790 decade were put to good use by Sade. Thus we find that
Adelaïde and Bathilde are forced to weave the rope which is to hang
them, and we watch as they prepare their own tombs (15:123–25).
Their sole means of escape is complicity with Stolbach, who has
short, deformed legs, long arms, the ears of an ape, and the face of
a dog (15:133). When Frederick wanders through the cemetery at
Brixen, lightning bolts flash around him, the earth trembles and
graves are laid open (15:189). The Italy visited by Adelaïde becomes
as sinister as the Germany which she had fled; she is given the
severed head of Antoine as a reminder not to become involved in
the politics of Venice (15:197). Finally, the secluded convent in
which the inhabitants are absorbed with death (15:220–25) is worthy of any gothic romance. These diabolic aspects are the redeeming
features of *Adelaïde de Brunswick*. They allow us to overlook some
of the weaker technical points of Sade's last works of fiction, and
to witness one of the new directions in fiction after 1800. The
portrayal of the lecherous Théodore de Gange is both Sadian and
gothic. The radical embellishment of the story of the queen of France
at the end of the fourteenth century is a rich mixture of history·and
Sadian immorality. While the old theme of virtue persecuted remains in *Adelaïde de Brunswick,* the emphasis is moved to the newer
elements of the grotesque, the suspenseful, and the supernatural.

Portraits of the Sadian Woman in 1800–1812

Since women are the center of attention of Sade's fiction, and
since images of women have been completely redefined in the recent
past, a brief analysis of his system of portraying them appears to be

justified. If we return briefly to the extended description of Isabelle of Bavaria, we recall that Sade's *portrait moral* of this notorious person was indicative of her political aims and personal inclinations, at least in the Sadian adaptation of her. He sought to have this woman stand out as the "grande gore" of the latter part of the Hundred Years' War, so that as a historian he could identify a specific cause for the evils which beset France at that time. Such detailed description and character development are quite exceptional in Sade's work. Since most of his women are victims, their portrayals are usually extremely brief; they are so uniform and so rigid in details given that one might say that each time a woman is introduced by the author, she will be attacked shortly thereafter.

A typical example of Sade's system of portraying women is found in *Adelaïde de Brunswick:*

Like almost all of the princesses of Germany, Adelaïde was tall and enchantingly shaped, with as much grace as dignity in her manners and as much delicacy as intelligence in her mind. Naturally made to command respect, she elicited that more often than love; but this respect was a part of the totality of her appearance, whereas the details were the realm of love. She was imposing by her manners and seductive by her soft ways; and beyond all that, there was something so tender and romantic in her features that when one looked at her, one was uncertain as to the type of homage which should be paid to her; but realizing that she should be exalted as the gods, she eventually won adoration as their finest creation. (15:84)

In this portrait, Sade emphasized the unsurpassed nature of Adelaïde's charm, the reactions which she is likely to provoke in men (notably respect), and the divine nature of her beauty. We see that she is tall, as we assume most German princesses are; but distinctive details of hair and eye color, dominant features or other particulars of the heroine are omitted. While claiming to be a "painter" of women's pictures, Sade was extremely pressed to arrive at the actions which would harm the subject of the painting.

The same elevation-degradation pattern continues in the description of Euphrasie de Gange. Her description is also transparent and devoid of graphic detail. We learn that Euphrasie, then Madame de Castellane, "soon earned the title of the most beautiful woman of the century" (11:191), and that "Madame de Castellane was rightfully considered as the most beautiful woman in France." Such optimum praise appears justified by other accounts of the Marquise de Gange, and is remindful of Mme. de La Fayette's description of Mlle. de Chartres in *La Princesse de Clèves,* a work which merited special praise in Sade's "Idée sur les romans." In addition to the obvious parallels between Mme. de la Fayette's novel and Sade's *Marquise de Gange* (unique beauty of the heroine, a weak husband, pursuit by and eventual rejection of the suitor), Béatrice Didier lists other important analogies between the two novels: the "dialectique du dévoilement," the "parole interdite," and the impossibility to communicate, all of which led to the final disintegration of the world of the Princesse de Clèves.[18]

The portraits of women in *Les Crimes de l'amour* follow the pattern described above.[19] The typical portrait here consists of a few lines, but no more than a paragraph. An appropriate example is the description of Henriette in "Miss Henriette Stralson":

> It was not surprising, moreover, that Miss Stralson could have arranged everything to her advantage at Ranelagh [a former resort area near London] when, together with an enchanting figure, the sweetest and most seductive eyes, the most beautiful hair in the world, the most delicate of features as well as the most spirited, one added a delightful tone of voice, much intelligence, kindness, and vivacity moderated by an air of modesty and virtue which made these charms even more distinguishable . . . and all of that at age seventeen. (10:132–33)

The heroines from the remaining tales of *Les Crimes de l'amour* differ only slightly from this norm. A few have lily-white skin, a reflection of their purity (Mlle. de Faxelange and Florville); some have, like Henriette, seductive eyes (Florinde in "Rodrigue"); and a number of them are "faite à peindre" (Ernestine, Amélie de Sancerre, and Mme. de Franval). For the most part, they are quite young, rather tall, and of fair complexion; thereafter, they are developed in terms of their actions toward others and those of others toward them. We have seen in *Les Crimes de l'amour,* the historical novels, and elsewhere that these actions can be most brutal. It was as though Sade attempted to elevate feminine beauty to rest momentarily on a pedestal, and then have it come crashing down immediately afterward. By this pattern, the most beautiful Marquise de Gange is subjected to a series of tortures, all designed to murder her. Henriette Stralson submits to multiple assaults by Granwel; and Ernestine is killed by her father, as planned by her ravisher Oxtiern. The only women to escape the cyclical pattern of beauty and murder are the harlots who are not described in any greater detail: Cécile in "Dorgeville" and Eugénie de Franval.

One could generalize to a certain extent and say that the women in Sade's writings of the final decade of his life were continuations of his two most famous caricatures, Justine and Juliette. The analogy is valid to a point. Justine lacks identity and is of little interest in herself, but is distinguished by the long succession of misfortunes brought against her, that is, the *vertus vexées*. From the paucity of concrete detail given about her, we merely assume that she can and does attract numerous aggressors to her. Juliette is equally unidentifiable, but forges an identity through the opposite means; she takes shape by her physical and moral outrages, and by her discourse thereon. As with Justine, we assume that she is attractive enough to draw a multitude of lechers to her. These extremes in feminine behavior are simultaneously present in one tale, "Eugénie de Franval." Before her disastrous marriage, Mme. de Franval (then Mlle. de Farneille) was described in a dozen lines or so as having a "delicious physiognomy," a virgin face, blond hair, a thin figure, lily-like skin, and so on (10:426–27). The delicate Mme. de Franval will be humiliated during the remainder of her existence. Her satanic daughter Eugénie is not described at any length, but instead acquires her identity through her relationship with her father. She is designed to wreak havoc in the lives of those who surround her. Since she was not defined like her mother, she is freer to pursue her libertine career.

In the tales of *Les Crimes de l'amour* Sade refers to himself as a painter and artist, with comments on his brushes and the colors used in his paintings.[20] In his preface to this collection ("Idée sur les romans"), after stressing the need for the infernal aspect of human existence and for *élans* from the writer, the theorist of the novel treated his craft with similar terms such as brushes and brush strokes, portraits, sketches, nuances, and hues (10:14–19). The novelist, who had previously assumed the role of chronicler in detailing the lives of past historical characters, added a new dimension to the art of fiction, that of the plastic arts. The same perspective is found in the introduction to *Aline et Valcour,* where Sade cautions us that the frightening traits of the letters which follow have never been witnessed before. Did Sade genuinely conceive of himself as a painter? Probably not, but he returns to the painting motif with striking frequency. In "Laurence et Antonio," the heroine (Laurence) transcribes in her own blood Petrarch's sonnet 57 (the portrait of Laura), so that she may preserve it for her imprisoned lover Antonio (10:309). At the end of the same tale, the author cites a comparison between painting and poetry (10:315–16). In *La Marquise de Gange,* we learn that the Marquis ordered a portrait of Euphrasie to be sent from Paris to his estate, and "it was this same portrait, that of the mother of the poor, which was worshipped by those who believed that they saw a goddess in it" (11:198). Similarly, when Théodore de Gange arrives, he announces that he too possesses a portrait of Euphrasie which was sent to him by his brother, and that it was the portrait which caused him to fall in love with her (11:207). The first portrait in question seems to have been authentic. According to Béatrice Didier, the real Marquise de Ganges served as a model for the celebrated portraitist Mignard when he painted the *Martyrdom of St. Roseline.*[21] Sade's legal confidant, the Président de Brosses, viewed Mignard's portrait in 1739, and wrote of its ravishing beauty and how he would have wished to martyrize the subject himself. Sade was to have seen the same portrait; and since the Marquise de Gange was predestined for martyrdom, he thus came upon the source of inspiration for his novel.

In spite of the insistence on painting and genuine portraits, one element is missing in the Sadian portraits of women. It is the concrete, distinctive feature or detail which would allow those otherwise faceless, victimized women to stand apart; it is the "verrue" sought by Diderot in the plastic arts and which he applied to his portrait of the lesbian mother superior in *La Religieuse.*[22] When Sade does provide a vivid detail, it is so distorted that it cannot be plausible: a huge clitoris in the case of his harlots; a seven-foot giant (Minski) who devours all that he rapes; in *La Philosophie dans le boudoir* a gardener Augustin with an enormous phallus, but without any other identity. The portraits of Sade's males are comparable in their superficiality to those of his females (for example, Franval). One exception is the description of Valcour, which is most likely that of Sade himself.

The rigidity of Sade's portrayal of women implies a passivity which eventually and consistently results in their victimization. When we first make the acquaintance of Mlle. de Florville, we expect that the soft and delicate whiteness of her skin, the rosy coolness of her mouth, and the molded shape of her limbs, together with the piety of her behavior (10:210), are features which will do more for her than to precipitate her cataclysmic destruction at the end; the haste with which these details are given corresponds to the rapidity of disastrous revelations at the conclusion of the tale. A portrait is displayed with the implicit purpose of mutilating it. The theory of the writer as portraitist is therefore at odds with Sade's practice, as is that of the role of *moraliste* who claims to extol virtue by painting vice. Did Sade know women at all, and hate them at the same time? Was he only the abuser of faceless prostitutes, seeking revenge because of the prudish nature of Mme. de Sade? The language used to qualify his portraits is that of painting, but it fails to lend credibility to the heroines of his short stories and late novels. Sade clings to the *Justine* syndrome, which was successful in 1788, but which tends toward exhaustion in 1800 and beyond. The absence of requited love and the image of women as objects debilitate Sade's characterizations. As Klossowski indicates, Sade was confronted with a dialectic contradiction which was to last his entire life.[23]

Chapter Seven
Sade and His Critics

Sade in the Nineteenth Century

The preceding commentaries on Sade's works serve to explain why he created more of a sensation and attracted greater notoriety, some justified, some unjustified, than any of his contemporaries. While most people today have heard of Voltaire and Rousseau, few have any familiarity with Montesquieu and Diderot, and only specialists and academics discuss Marivaux, Prévost, and Laclos. Almost everyone, however, has heard of the Marquis de Sade, but few have read his books.

Sade's last three contributions to literature, the trilogy of historical novels, did not attract much attention, a fact that is quite understandable when one recalls that two of them remained unpublished until 1953–54. But Sade's reputation had already been fixed at the turbulent conclusion of the eighteenth century, and we have seen ample proof of its "infamous" nature. Furthermore, when we compare the literary trends which dominated the first part of the nineteenth century to the content of Sadian fiction, we can readily understand the relative silence on him before 1860. Although the restored Bourbon regime and the July monarchy were not as overtly stifling as their counterparts in England, they were no more receptive to Sade's intensity than revolutionary Paris had been. Claude Duchet's article, "L'Image de Sade à l'époque romantique," explains Sade's anonymity for almost fifty years.[1] Other than the 1834 study by Jules Janin on Sade, which was condemnatory and which drew enough public attention to justify a separate reprint, the Marquis de Sade was relegated to infrequent quips and references in journals and personal diaries. Such is the case with Benjamin Constant, who observed in a note in his *Journal intime* in 1804: "The novel *Justine* is not in the least an exaggeration of human corruption."[2] Curiously, Sade himself had foreseen the unflattering treatment which his best work would receive when, together with the name of his nemesis Villeterque, he cited those of Mme. de Genlis, Chateaubriand, and

La Harpe in his *Notes littéraires*.[3] In 1840, the young Flaubert recommended to Ernest Chevalier: "Read the Marquis de Sade and read him to the last page of the last volume; that will complete your moral education."[4] In contrast, Stendhal limited himself to several uncomplimentary associations between Sade, Eugène Sue, and François Cenci, in 1834.[5]

A few years later, Sainte-Beuve, one of the greatest literary critics of them all, published an item entitled "Quelques vérités sur la situation en littérature" in the *Revue des deux mondes*. After citing traces of Sade's influence on several writers of the period, Sainte-Beuve set forth this observation: "I dare ascertain, without fear of being contradicted, that Byron and Sade—and I beg forgiveness for the association—are perhaps the two greatest sources of inspiration for our moderns, the first being ostensibly visible, the second clandestine, but not too clandestine."[6] Sainte-Beuve's judgment is astute for two reasons: its date (1 July 1843) marks the beginning of an increase in visibility for Sade, and second, his presence in the latter part of the nineteenth century and the first decades of the twentieth century was felt primarily among poets. The most frequently cited instance is that of Algernon Swinburne, who came to know Sade through the intermediary of Lord Houghton, the latter having provided the poet with pornographic works of all kinds, including some by Sade. In a letter to Houghton of July 1865, Swinburne recognized his debt to the French author: "The poet, thinker and man of the world from whom the theology of my poem ["Atalanta"] is derived was greater than Byron. . . . He indeed, fatalist or not, saw to the bottom of gods and men."[7] Swinburne also wrote a long poem in French, "Charenton en 1810" (written in 1861, published in 1951), and an "Apologie de Sade," also in French (written in 1916, printed for private circulation).[8]

It is among the poets of the latter nineteenth century that one would expect to find the greatest recognition of Sade's importance, and such is precisely the case with Baudelaire and Verlaine. Baudelaire, the father of modern poetry who emphasized sensations and sensitivity, the diabolic and the occult in his unprecedented and unrivaled verse, did not dwell at any length on his debt to Sade. In his "Projets et Notes diverses," however, he wrote one memorable sentence: "One must always come back to Sade, by that I mean to *Natural Man,* in order to explain evil."[9] Verlaine was more explicit, in four lines from the poem "A Gabriel Vicaire":

I am a sensualist, you are another.
But you, gentle, riant, a Gaulois and a half.
While I am the shadow of the Marquis de Sade, and this I am
Among the occasional false and naive airs of a good apostle.

Verlaine's personal anxieties and sexual frustrations and eccentricities cannot be totally attributed to his reading the Marquis de Sade; the same can be said of Swinburne. We prefer to think that some of the more refined literary and philosophical aspects of his volumes were involved in the process of influencing later authors, but detailed studies of this type of influence have yet to be done.

Sade in the Twentieth Century

The poets of the first part of the twentieth century continued to stress the importance of the Marquis de Sade in the formation of their literary ideas and their manner of expression. This applies to the most unique poet of the first two decades of this century, Guillaume Apollinaire, who was directly responsible for resurrecting Sade. In 1909, Apollinaire prefaced a partial edition of Sade, *L'Oeuvre du Marquis de Sade, pages choisies,* with a fifty-seven-page essay entitled "Le Divin Marquis." In it, he wrote a biographical sketch of Sade, provided synopses of his major writings, corrected the denunciations and misconceptions of Sade which had surfaced in the preceding century, and concluded with a citation from Sade: "I address myself only to people capable of understanding me, and these people will read me without danger."[10] Apollinaire's approach to Sade inaugurated a positive trend that has continued to the present. We have already indicated the 1904 edition of *Les 120 Journées de Sodome* by Iwan Bloch, which associated Sade with Krafft-Ebing and his *Psychopathia sexualis.* The positive trend was pursued foremost by two scholars, Gilbert Lely and Maurice Heine, whose efforts resulted in several major editions of Sade's works and included a wealth of material previously unedited. Lely was so taken with the importance of Sade and so obsessed with his efforts at restoring him to dignity that he reputedly left a place setting, albeit a vacant one, for Sade at his dining table. His encyclopedic contributions to Sade studies culminate with a poem, "Sade," and which concludes thus:

We believe in the revolt of Rimbaud, in that of Lautréamont and of Sade.

We believe in the value of Poetry, of Love and of Liberty.
We believe in the Surrealist Revolution.[11]

Paperback editions of Sade continue to appear regularly in France, notably in the *10/18* series. The 1957 Pauvert edition of Sade's opus, and the ensuing trial which ended in the deletion of the more controversial writings, are symptomatic of the continually troubled reception of the "Divine Marquis" by the public. Regarding that trial, one should at least mention that testimony in favor of the unexpurgated publication of Sade was given by writers such as Georges Bataille, André Breton, Jean Cocteau, and Jean Paulhan. The indebtedness of Breton and other poets to Sade antedates 1957 by many years, however. Sade was indeed the "Right Person for Surrealism."[12] Emphasizing revolt, nihilism, and a search for new orientations in art by means of outrage and shock tactics, these writers appropriately singled out Sade as one of their apostles. In the first *Manifeste du Surréalisme* (1924), Breton included Sade in his famous enumeration of precursors: Sade was "surrealistic in Sadism," as Swift was in mischief, Chateaubriand in exoticism, and soon. In the second *Manifeste* (1930), Breton eulogized Sade again for the perfect integrity of his thought and life. He continued to praise Sade in his *Anthologie de l'humour noir,* and later made it known that the "Exposition inteRnatiOnale du Surréalisme, 1959–1960" had been organized under the aegis of the Marquis de Sade.[13]

Other members of the surrealist group continued the homage which Breton paid to Sade. René Char published a "Homage à D. A. F. de Sade" in 1931, and identified Sade and Lautréamont as the cornerstones of his system of thought. Similarly, Paul Eluard explained Sade's insistence on virtue punished as an effort to return man to his primitive instincts, as opposed to the respect of traditional Christian values, which only perpetuated moral enslavement (*Evidence poétique,* 1939). Sade's name and his radical literature entered not only the polemical writings of dadaism and surrealism; he also penetrated the realm of painting. René Magritte executed an interpretation of *La Philosophie dans le boudoir,* and Man Ray painted a stylized portrait of Sade in which the rugged stones of the Bastille fortress are blended into the subject's face. (Ray's painting is the frontispiece to this study.)

The specific questions of direct influence by Sade on modern writers, both French and non-French, are yet to be answered. One

of the more obvious areas where such influence should be found is
in the theatrical writings of Antonin Artaud; according to Ronald
Hayman, Artaud's idea for a Theater of Cruelty was based on Sade's
principles.[14] But before a comprehensive account can be made of
the degree of Sade's penetration into the ideas and expressions of
major contemporary writers, we must content ourselves with occasional manifestations of indebtedness. Such is the case with Albert
Camus who, like Baudelaire, briefly but poignantly acknowledged
the importance of Sade: "With him really began the history and
the tragedy of our times."[15] Aldous Huxley's evaluation of Sade is
almost identical. In his note on Sade in *Ends and Means,* he wrote:
"De Sade's philosophy was the philosophy of meaninglessness carried
to its logical conclusion. Life was without significance. . . . His
books are of permanent interest and value because they contain a
kind of *reductio ad absurdum* of revolutionary theory. . . . De Sade
is the only completely consistent and thorough-going revolutionary
of history."[16] When one recalls the pessimistic social and political
atmosphere of 1930–40, one can appreciate why the name of Sade
was quoted in this manner by Huxley and Camus.

More recently, two leaders of the *nouveau roman* phenomenon of
the 1950–60 period contributed essays on Sade: Alain Robbe-Grillet
and André Pieyre de Mandiargues.[17] Sade has even been commem-
orated in film. Luis Buñuel's 1930 surrealist film, *L'Age d'or,* contains a scene derived from *Les 120 Journées de Sodome.* In that scene,
the Duc de Blangis appears as a Christ-like figure who offers help
to a young girl. For this scene and others, the film elicited such a
scandal that it was withdrawn from public circulation in 1934.
Similar to the 1957 trial of the Pauvert company, the surrealists
circulated a questionnaire defending the Buñuel film; it was signed
by Aragon, Breton, Char, Dali, Eluard, Ernst, Man Ray, Tzara,
and others. In 1975, the Italian cinema director Pasolini produced
a film entitled *Salo, ou les 120 Journées de Sodome.* As one can easily
imagine, the life and legend of the Marquis de Sade have also fostered
the production of a series of x-rated films (*Justine, De Sade*).

One of the most penetrating accounts written on Sade by modern
authors is Simone de Beauvoir's *Faut-il brûler Sade?* Together with
the insights mentioned previously in the course of this study, Beauvoir compares Sade's biographic and literary situation to that of
Oscar Wilde, another author whose personal behavior and writings
were viewed as being so outrageous that public humiliation and

ruin were the results.[18] The case of Wilde shows that even one hundred years after Sade, unconventional private behavior, when made public (what is labeled *outrage aux moeurs* in France), can entail the most dire of consequences for an author.

Since 1945, the number of books and articles written on Sade has multiplied rapidly, each year witnessing dozens of essays, commemorative issues in serials, and books. It is no mere coincidence that some of the most perceptive and most highly regarded analyses of him have been from the structuralist point of view. The cyclical nature of Sade's fiction, his verbal aggression, and the need to say all about the previously ineffable, make Sade a likely candidate for such an approach. As indicated in the discussion of Sade's philosophical treatises, the structuralist psychologist Jacques Lacan was the first to point out the kinship between Kant's *Critique of Practical Reason* and Sade's thought, and the relationship between crime and pleasure derived therefrom. Roland Barthes, in his essay "L'Arbre du crime" (in the winter 1967 edition of *Tel Quel* devoted to Sade), and in his *Sade, Fourier, Loyola,* used a topical approach to identify the significance of *things* in Sade's linguistic system: food, clothing, mirrors, among others. Pierre Klossowski has been cited twice in the course of this study. If we had to reduce his abundant criticism on Sade to several cardinal points, they would be the following: (1) the relationships between the Sadian conscience, God, and fellowman are negative, but to the extent that these negations are real, they introduce the very notions which they suppress; without the notions of God and fellowman as points of attack, there can be no Sadian conscience; (2) Sade's use of the word *vertu,* as is amply done in *Justine, La Nouvelle Justine,* and *Juliette,* does not automatically translate as its closest equivalent "virtue," but rather as a primordial virginity which is the focus of Sadian oppression; (3) the idea of *delectatio morosa,* that is, the desire for death by those who are incapable of finding it, is frequently manifested in Sadian characters, and again, a seemingly negative exponent becomes a positive, creative one.[19]

Two other critics of structuralist affiliation have contributed significantly to our understanding of Sade today. Georges Bataille, who testified at the Pauvert trial in 1957, prefaced *La Nouvelle Justine* with an essay, "Sade et l'homme normal" (6:45–65). Like Barthes and Klossowski, Bataille concentrates on Sade's *langage;* using *La Philosophie dans le boudoir* as his point of reference, Bataille arrives at a different conclusion. Since the language of normal men opposes the expression of violence, violence itself must be suspended when the discursive element of Sade assumes priority, and the resultant situation is, as illustrated in *La Philosophie dans le boudoir* (and in all of Sade's other extreme works), the dual structure of action (sex) interrupted by lengthy philosophical discourse. According to Bataille, Sade's language is more than that of a man revolting against confinement or against a few particulars; it is an assault against all of humanity.[20]

The only major nineteenth-century writer not examined previously and who felt the influence of Sade is Lautréamont (Isadore Ducasse). In another monumental work of Sadian criticism, *Lautréamont et Sade* (1963), Maurice Blanchot is less preoccupied with the question of direct influence than with affinities between the two, although he does list obvious areas of influence.[21] Like Philippe Sollers, in his 1967 *Tel Quel* article "Sade dans le texte," Blanchot concentrates on a passage of vital importance in *Juliette,* where Clairwil offers her definition of the perfect crime:

I would like, said Clairwil, to find a crime whose everlasting effect would continue to act, even when I would no longer be acting, so that there would not be one single moment in my life, even when asleep, during which I would not be the cause of some disturbance, and this disturbance could extend to the point of causing general corruption or so formal a disruption that its effect would be prolonged beyond the limit of my life. (8:503).

To this desire of the utopian, self-perpetuating crime, Juliette responds: "In order to complete this project, my angel, I responded, I see few alternatives other than what can be called moral assassination, which is realized through counsel, through writing, or through action" (8:503). From this and other *élans* of verbal rebellion, we can see why Sade has had a captive audience among recent critics and why, as early as 1909, writers like Apollinaire spoke of Juliette as a new woman with "wings" who breaks loose from the rest of humanity (see chapter 3). Sade's depictions of human sexuality, femininity, and masculinity are at times as credible as Lautréamont's hero Maldoror, who copulates with a female shark. We have already seen that to the extent that Sade was fascinated with feminine beauty, his numerous portraits of women pose many problems of credibility. Sade's violence is indeed that of language. If he were interpreted literally, there would be no survivors left to read him.

For these and other reasons, it is not surprising that the majority of studies on Sade which have appeared in the last few years have been authored primarily by women. The problem of cruelty to women in his fiction is bound to provoke reactions of one form or another. The studies mentioned in preceding chapters (those of Laborde, Didier, Fink, Gallop, and Lee) are not necessarily feminist criticisms; nor are they merely "corrected" views of Sade's treatment of women. Alice Laborde has traced the evolution of Sade's most famous work from the draft of *Les Infortunes de la vertu* through the definitive *Justine* and *La Nouvelle Justine,* and has also shown that to the degree that the text is amplified, its plausibility decreases.[22] Béatrice Didier has explained the nature and function of the *château intérieur* motif in Sade's principal works.[23] One can expect many more interpretations of Sade by women in the coming years.

Dictionaries and biographies have a rather significant role in determining the manner in which an author becomes known to the general public. In the third chapter of this study, the hostility against Sade of Michaud's *Biographie universelle* was noted, and even against the relatively innocuous texts *Aline et Valcour* and *Isabelle de Bavière.* The publication date of Michaud's biography (1854) shows that its negativity corresponds to the generally hostile reception of Sade at that time. The *Petit Larousse* dictionary is probably the most popular of all French dictionaries. Its encyclopedic section contained no entry on Sade until 1935. That particular edition tersely introduced Sade with: "Sade (Marquis de), famous for his morbidly obscene novels, born in Paris (1740–1814)."[24] The *Petit Larousse* entries on Sade improved commensurately with his restoration to dignity through the efforts of writers cited in the preceding paragraphs. The 1969 version of the same dictionary was remarkably more favorable to Sade; its entry, which remained virtually unchanged until 1980, read: "Sade (D. A. F., Marquis de) French writer, born in Paris (1740–1814). His novels depict characters obsessed with the demonic pleasure of making innocent victims suffer, but the importance of his works derives from his presentation therein of the revolt of free men against God and society." Even the reservations concerning demonic cruelty and the persecution of the innocent have disappeared in the revised 1981 edition of the same popular dictionary: "Sade (Marquis de). French writer born in Paris (1740–1814). His work, which is both the theory and illustration of sadism, constitutes the pathological double of naturalist and liberal philosophies of the Age of Enlightenment."[25] This newest entry goes so far as to cite two of Sade's creations, *Justine* and *La Philosophie dans le boudoir*. The gradual evolution in the entries from a mass-distributed dictionary may seem to be a trivial detail, but it also demonstrates the general ideological progress made in Sade commentaries.

"Homme de lettres": such was the only title for which Sade expressed any interest, and the one by which he wanted to be remembered. The dossier of his complete works, begun in 1789, was arranged under the heading "Portefeuille d'un homme de lettres." The title "Marquis" was of little importance to him; at times, it was a political liability, and then as now it had a pejorative aura about it. In the seventeenth century, the word was used as the equivalent of fop; today, the complete title "Marquis de Sade" still conjurs up negative implications of sadism and masochism. The proletarian "Louis" Sade, as he signed his papers in 1790–1800, was even less desirable, and only occasionally did the aristocratic particle *de* reappear in Sade's letters after 1800. It was not as an aristocrat nor as the founding father of perversion that Sade thought of himself, but as a writer. In fact, his last will and testament, which he drafted in 1806, expresses a remarkable humility:

I absolutely forbid that my body be viewed for any reason whatsoever. . . . Once my grave is filled in, it will be seeded with acorns, so that the dirt of the said grave will eventually hold vegetation, and once the thicket is grown back to its original state, the traces of my grave will disappear from the face of the earth, just as I hope that my memory will be erased from the minds of men, except for the small number of them who chose to love me until the end and whose sweet memory I will take to my resting place.(2:632)

These are not the words of a madman interned in the Charenton insane asylum. Dr. Royer-Collard's testimony of 1808 indicates that Sade was in full possession of his wits at the end of his life—a fact which is further attested in his own letters of the period. The judgments of insanity professed against Sade are based on associations with the institution itself and its other internees.

Ironically, Sade's request for eternal oblivion was not respected. Some years after his death, Sade's remains were accidentally exhumed and his skull was submitted to a phrenologist named Spurzheim who, instead of finding indications of a belligerent or perverted man, found characteristics of "benevolence and religious faith."[26]

Obviously, Sade's letters do not have the historical or literary significance of the correspondence of Voltaire or that of Rousseau, for example. But the almost three hundred of his letters which have survived deal with a vast range of subjects and temperaments, and include satire, parody, and scatology. They are an accurate source of reflections of the real man. His correspondence was submitted to a fate which recalls that of many of his other writings; it was published for the first time in 1929 by Paul Bourdin, who disdainfully qualified the letters with the remark: "I never succeed in taking him [Sade] seriously."[27] Gilbert Lely eventually produced a more complete and more reliable edition of these letters. Those of the beginning of Sade's first long period of incarceration (1777–90) witness the agony of imprisonment: "Never . . . has my blood or my mind been able to bear total confinement" (12:112). His protests against isolation recall the grim despair of the victims of Ste.-Marie-des-bois: "I am alone here, I am at the limit of the world, removed from all eyes, without any creature ever being able to reach me" (13:207). Sade's complex system of numerically encoded messages to his wife has already been noted, as well as his admission of libertinism in his "grande lettre" written to Mme. de Sade in 1781. That letter, written amid the frustration due to confinement and the intense hostility toward his persecutors, is a masterpiece of candor and lyric expression. After giving his version of the public scandals prior to 1776 and after admitting that he was a libertine, but not a criminal or a murderer, Sade concludes:

There you have a very long letter, do you not? But I owed it to myself, and promised myself that I would write it on the anniversary of my four years of suffering. They have elapsed. There it is, written as if I were at the point of death, so that if [death] should surprise me without having the consolation of holding you once more in my arms, I could remind you in dying of the feelings expressed in this letter. . . . I will not ask you to respond to me in detail, but only that you tell me that you have received my *grande lettre;* that is how I will name it. And when I recall to you the sentiments which it contains, you will reread it. . . . Do you understand, my dear? You will reread it and see that he who will love you until the grave wanted to sign it in his own blood. (12:278)

Perhaps writing was the "perfect crime" for the Marquis de Sade, as he had Juliette observe so bluntly. Since he already faced indefinite isolation for debaucheries which were left unpunished when others of his stature committed them, and since the ire and disgrace felt by his mother-in-law was continued by his own family, he could not be punished any further, and spent the two decades following 1781 writing books which provoke the most vociferous reactions today. His personal letters of the 1790–1800 period show only that he was obsessed with survival and monetary solvency—a trait which may explain the scope and intensity of *La Nouvelle Justine* and *Juliette*. In the final stage of his imprisonment (1802–14), he was still denying the authorship of *Justine,* the point of departure for the pornographic expansions mentioned (12:597) and concentrated mainly on obtaining official pardon. But the image of Sade as the author of the "infamous" *Justine* was so firmly established even then that the remark which he flippantly made to his lawyer Gaufridy in 1775, that "not one cat will be beaten in the province without people saying: *it was the Marquis de Sade,*" remains fairly valid for his reception by posterity.

Chapter Eight
Conclusion

From his earliest writings, Sade was on the attack. He protested against the conventional belief in God and against conventional morality. His *élans,* which he recommended for all writers, challenged political order and taboos, and fostered blasphemy, robbery, rape, and even murder. Through writing, he found that crime whose everlasting effect would resound throughout the world long after his departure.

Other French writers of Sade's time were imprisoned for the audacity and extremism of their ideas (Voltaire, Marmontel, Diderot). Some (for example, Rousseau) saw the burning of their controversial books. But Sade was initially confined for what appears to be, at the onset, a trivial detail: the wrath of his mother-in-law; and he was kept in prison by the continuing power of *lettres de cachet.* Even the total reversal of values of the French Revolution did not free him from the force of the past.

Some of the signs of a great writer are diversity, recognition of quality in other writers, and admiration by posterity. As we have seen, Sade was prolific and diverse. He practiced many forms of the novel; he wrote dozens of dramas and short stories, and even some verse; and he added epic dimensions to his masterpiece, *Justine.* The acutely pornographic nature of these expansions (*La Nouvelle Justine* and *Juliette*) are explained, but not necessarily excused, by the fact that Sade desperately needed money to live at the time. Sade borrowed from the main philosophical currents of his epoch and, with varying degrees of success, adapted the ideas of La Mettrie, Voltaire, and Rousseau to his own system. The final chapter shows that he generated the greatest interest among writers who were also revolutionary for their time.

Times have changed, and moral standards have evolved. If one work typifies the nature of Sade's literature, it would have to be *Justine.* It was considered infamous for its day, but is hardly infamous by modern criteria. Nonetheless, those who have read *Justine* will never forget the fate ascribed to the heroine, after her life of numerous attempts to adhere to traditional morality. Those who have ventured into the clandestine and unfinished chronicle of *Les 120 Journées de Sodome* will remember that for each horror committed, greater ones await. Thirty years of imprisonment do not explain the Marquis de Sade's opus. But the cycle of imprisonment and persecution is the essence of his theater, tales, and best known works.

Sade's revolt goes beyond the usual paradoxes and *remises en question* of values by other writers of his time. Yet he leaves us with unanswered questions and contradictions. If revolt is to be the new order of things, what follows? His closed sphere of operations can succeed for only a small number of oppressors. The earliest lesson from the boudoir was the defilement of all that is sacred, and the rejection of that which was previously valued. If it is natural to pursue limitless pleasure, what is the nature of those who are forced to participate? If feminine beauty is of any value, how can it be continually destroyed? Sade does not answer all of these questions. Like his victims, we are left alone to resolve them. But our judgments of him should be based on contact with the complete spectrum of his ideas and abilities, and not merely on automatic reflexes to the mention of the "Marquis de" Sade, infamy, insanity, sadism, or masochism.

Notes and References

Chapter One

1. The edition of Sade's works used throughout this study is the *Oeuvres complètes* prepared by Gilbert Lely in the Tête de Feuilles edition, 16 volumes in 8 (Paris, 1973). It is based on, but should not be confused with, the Gallimard edition of Sade's works, printed in 1950–57. The Tête de Feuilles edition is, however, the same in editing and pagination as the Cercle du Livre précieux version of Sade's *Oeuvres complètes* (Paris, 1966–67). The Tête de Feuilles edition includes Lely's complete biography of Sade (vol. 1) as well as the major critical studies written to that date. It is this edition that is cited in the text. Unless otherwise indicated, all translations are mine.

2. See Maurice Heine's description of Saumane in *Le Marquis de Sade* (Paris, 1950), pp. 331–34.

3. *Aline et Valcour,* in *Oeuvres complètes,* 2:letter 5.

4. *Oeuvres complètes,* 1:57–64.

5. See, for example, Ronald Hayman, *De Sade: A Critical Biography* (New York, 1978), p. 81.

6. See Sade's *Correspondance,* in *Oeuvres complètes,* 12:259, 394.

7. Such speculation is based on an isolated remark by Renée-Pélagie in a letter to Gaufridy dated 29 July 1774.

8. Heine, *Le Marquis de Sade,* pp. 155–210.

9. Lely, *Sade* (Paris: Gallimard, 1967), p. 52.

10. Heine, *Le Marquis de Sade,* pp. 203–4.

11. According to Donald Thomas, the cantharide candies were also known as "pastilles de Richelieu," since they were used frequently by the Duc de Richelieu. The concubines introduced to Louis XV were also reported to have eaten them. See D. Thomas, *The Marquis de Sade* (Boston, 1976), pp. 74–75.

12. My account of this episode is based on Lely's documentation in *Oeuvres complètes,* 1:548 ff.

13. See the letter dictated by Sade to l'abbé de Sade, and written by his wife, in which he reminds his uncle of the latter's own past debaucheries, and strongly urges cooperation (*Oeuvres complètes,* 12:70 ff.).

14. The reference is to Béatrice Didier, *Sade: une écriture du désir* (Paris, 1976), p. 80.

15. Geoffrey Gorer, *The Life and Ideas of the Marquis de Sade* (New York, 1962), p. 52.

16. Madame Roland, *Mémoires particuliers,* quoted in G. May, *L'Autobiographie* (Paris: Presses universitaires de France, 1979), p. 50.

17. Heine, *Le Marquis de Sade,* p. 255.

18. I refer to the "Projet de refonte de 1803–04," which concerns primarily his short stories and dramas.

19. Sade, *Journal inédit,* ed. G. Daumas (Paris: Gallimard, 1970), p. 134–35.

20. The Bettmann Archive possesses a picture of Sade, which is reproduced on the cover of the *Yale French Studies* issue (35 [1965]) devoted to Sade, but bears no date or artist's name.

21. Thomas, *The Marquis de Sade,* p. 150.

Chapter Two

1. Gorer, *Marquis de Sade,* pp. 100–106.

2. See my discussion of *Sainville et Léonore* in chapter 5.

3. Quoted by Lely in *Oeuvres complètes,* 2:244–45.

4. Virgil Topazio, *D'Holbach's Moral Philosophy* (Geneva: Institut Voltaire, 1956), pp. 120–38.

5. See Didier, *Sade,* Chap. 4, "Le Dialogue philosophique," pp. 41–57.

6. Vera Lee, "Innocence and Initiation in the Eighteenth-Century French Novel," *Studies on Voltaire and the Eighteenth Century* 153 (1976):1312.

7. *Oeuvres complètes,* 3:478–524.

8. Pierre Klossowski has devoted a comprehensive study to this essay, in the context of revolutionary developments. It is "Sade et la Révolution," and is reprinted in *Oeuvres complètes,* 4:349–65.

9. Roland Barthes, *Sade, Fourier, Loyola,* trans. Richard Miller (New York, 1976), p. 31.

10. *Oeuvres complètes,* 2:513.

11. Angela Carter, *The Sadeian Woman and the Ideology of Pornography* (New York: Pantheon, 1978), p. 91.

12. Joseph McMahon, "Where Does Real Life Begin?" *Yale French Studies* 35 (1965):99.

13. *Les 120 Journées de Sodome,* in *Oeuvres complètes,* 13:433.

14. *Oeuvres complètes,* 2:251–52.

15. Barthes, "L'Arbre du crime," *Tel Quel* 28 (Winter 1967):29.

16. See, for example, pt. 1, pp. 79–83.

17. Marcel Hénaff, *Sade: l'Invention du corps libertin* (Paris, 1978), p.

18. Lee, "The Sade Machine," *Studies on Voltaire and the Eighteenth Century* 98 (1972):210–11. The quotation is also found in Sade's *Oeuvres complètes,* 12:350.

19. For an example, see the description of Durcet in *Oeuvres complètes,* 13:19 and numerous other instances in parts 1–2 of *Les 120 Journées de Sodome.*

20. Richard Von Krafft-Ebing, *Psychopathia sexualis,* trans. Harry Wedeck (New York: Putnam, 1965), p. 13.

21. My remark is based on the standard edition of the *Complete Psychological Works of Sigmund Freud* (London: Hogarth, 1953–73).

22. Jane Gallop, "Sade, Mothers and Other Women," *Enclitic* 4, no. 2 (1981):60–68.

23. Jacques Lacan, "Kant avec Sade," *Critique* 191 (April 1963):291–313.

24. Ibid., pp. 300–301.

25. In his *Nature and Culture* (Baltimore: Johns Hopkins Press, 1963), Lester Crocker notes other inconsistencies in Sade's system of thought. See pp. 426–28 in particular.

26. Ann Thomson, "L'Art de Jouir de La Mettrie à Sade," in *Aimer en France, 1760–1860* (Clermont-Ferrand: Publications de la Faculté de lettres et de sciences humaines de Clermont-Ferrand, 1980), pp. 316–17.

27. Roger Lacombe, *Sade et ses masques* (Paris, 1974), p. 198.

Chapter Three

1. *Justine* is printed in volume 3 of Sade's *Oeuvres complètes.*

2. Quoted in Sade's *Journal inédit,* p. 135.

3. Barry Ivker, "On the Darker Side of the Enlightenment: A Comparison of the Literary Techniques of Sade and Restif," *Studies on Voltaire and the Eighteenth Century* 74 (1971):214.

4. Heine, *Le Marquis de Sade,* pp. 46–47. *Les Infortunes de la vertu* is reprinted in *Oeuvres complètes,* vol. 14.

5. Didier, *Sade,* p. 103.

6. Ibid., pp. 103–4.

7. Alice Laborde, *Sade romancier* (Neuchâtel, 1974), chap. 3, "Etude comparée de l'épisode de l'abbaye de Sainte-Marie dans les trois versions de *Justine,*" pp. 41–129.

8. Didier, *Sade,* pp. 98–99.

9. Jean Fabre, *Idées sur les romans, de Madame de Lafayette au Marquis de Sade* (Paris: Klincksieck, 1979), p. 168.

10. For a good treatment of Sade's readings of Scandinavian literature, see Lacombe, *Sade et ses masques,* chaps. 1–2.

11. Didier, *Sade,* pp. 85–86; Nancy Miller, "*Justine,* or the Vicious Circle," *Studies in Eighteenth-Century Culture* 5 (1976):217–18.

12. Ivker, "On the Darker Side," p. 200.

13. Didier, *Sade,* p. 106.

14. "Idée sur les romans."

15. Fougeret de Montbron, *Margot la ravaudeuse* (Paris: Pauvert, 1965), pp. 57–58. In *Juliette,* Sade gave a brief and farcical review of pornographical works of his time. He ridiculed *L'Académie des dames, l'Education de Laure,* and Gervaise de la Touche's *Portier des Chartreux,* and reserved modest praise and admiration for the Marquis d'Argens's *Thérèse philosophe* (*Juliette,* 8:442–43).

16. Maurice Blanchot, "Préface" to *La Nouvelle Justine* and *Juliette,* in *Oeuvres complètes,* 6:22.

17. *Juliette* is reprinted in *Oeuvres complètes,* vols. 8–9.

18. Kate Millet, *Sexual Politics* (New York: Ballantine, 1978), p. 410.

19. Jane Gallop, *Intersections: A Reading of Sade with Bataille, Blanchot and Klossowski* (Lincoln, 1981), p. 105.

20. For an example, see Juliette's account of the nature of her sexual excitement in 9:86.

21. Didier, *Sade,* p. 29 ff.

22. Millet, *Sexual Politics,* p. 43.

23. Germaine Greer, *The Female Eunuch* (New York: McGraw-Hill, 1971), pp. 82–92.

24. See also Roberta Hackel, *De Sade's Quantitative Moral Universe: of Irony, Rhetoric and Boredom* (The Hague: Mouton, 1976).

Chapter Four

1. The collection of *Historiettes, Contes et Fabliaux* is printed in volume 14 of Sade's *Oeuvres complètes. Les Crimes de l'amour* can be found in volume 10.

2. Heine, *Le Marquis de Sade,* p. 38.

3. "Projet de refonte de 1803–04," in *Oeuvres complètes,* 2:526–28. A third instance in which the two collections were blended is Sade's *Notes littéraires* of the 1803–4 period, in *Oeuvres complètes,* 15:32–33.

4. Heine, *Le Marquis de Sade,* p. 40.

5. A twenty-sixth tale, "Dorci," is characteristically omitted from the group entitled *Historiettes, Contes et Fabliaux.* "Dorci" was published separately by Anatole France, himself a *conteur* of considerable magnitude, in 1881.

6. Sade did not complete "La Marquise de Thélème," although it is printed in his *Oeuvres complètes.*

7. For further discussion of the autobiographical elements in "Le Président mystifié," see Thomas, *The Marquis de Sade,* pp. 166–68.

8. Baculard d'Arnaud was singled out for special praise by Sade in his "Idée sur les romans," 10:14.

9. See the "Projet d'Avertissement de l'auteur pour le recueil primitif des Contes et Nouvelles," in *Oeuvres complètes*, 10:497 ff.

10. To cite only one example, Boccaccio's second story of the seventh day of the *Decameron*, in which a wife puts her lover inside a barrel to hide him from her husband, closely resembles the scene mentioned in "Le Président mystifié" and the basic ploy found in "La Châtelaine de Longeville."

11. The quotations are taken from H. E. Bates, "The Modern Short Story: Retrospect," in *Short Story Theories*, ed. Charles E. May (Columbus: Ohio State University Press, 1976), p. 74.

12. See Murray Sachs, "The Emergence of a Poetics," in *The French Short Story*, University of South Carolina French Literature Series, vol. 2 (Columbia, 1975), pp. 139–51.

13. Richard Summers, *Craft of the Short Story* (New York: Rinehart, 1948), p. 24–27.

14. Although the "Idée sur les romans" was in fact the original preface of *Les Crimes de l'amour*, it concerns fiction in general much more than these short tales, and thus will be examined in chapter 5 of this study.

15. Didier, *Sade*, pp. 73–74.

16. Sade, *Notes littéraires*, in *Oeuvres complètes*, 15:37.

17. "Eugénie de Franval" is published in the Bibliothèque de la Pléiade, in *Romanciers du XVIIIᵉ siècle*, ed. R. Etiemble (Paris: Gallimard, 1965), vol. 2. Sade's other works contained in this volume are "Augustine de Villebranche," "Emilie de Tourville," "Il y a place pour deux," "Florville et Courval," and "Le Président mystifié."

18. The scene in question was restored to the complete edition of "Eugénie de Franval" by Maurice Heine.

19. Villeterque's attack on Sade was printed in the *Journal des arts, des sciences et de la littérature* in 1801 (see *Oeuvres complètes*, 2:520–23).

20. *Le Théâtre de Sade*, ed. Jean-Jacques Brochier, 4 vols. (Paris: Pauvert, 1970); references are designated by *Théâtre*, followed by the volume and page number.

21. See, for example, the prefaces to "Jeanne Laisné," "Les Jumelles," and "L'Union des arts."

22. Ironically, a similar disturbance occurred in March 1792 at the Théâtre italien, during the performance of Sade's "Le Suborneur." A Jacobine faction created a boisterous disturbance, because the play was written by an "aristocrat" (2:327–28).

23. The last two plays listed are not included in Brochier's presentation of "L'Union des arts." "La Tour enchantée" is printed separately, and "Cléontine" is not printed at all.

24. Peter Weiss, *The Persecution and Assassination of Jean-Paul Marat, as performed by the Inmates of the Asylum of Charenton, under the Direction of the Marquis de Sade* (New York: Pocket Books, 1971).

25. Ibid., p. 72.

Chapter Five

1. *Aline et Valcour* begins in vol. 4 of Sade's *Oeuvres complètes*. Sainville's digression is also printed in vol. 4; the story of Léonore continues in vol. 5, and the complete novel terminates there also. Since the novel is written in letter form, designations of particular letters are given after direct quotations.

2. Lely's *Notice* to *Aline et Valcour*, in *Oeuvres complètes*, 2:496.

3. Didier, preface to *Aline et Valcour* (Paris: Librairie générale de France, 1976), p. 5.

4. Simone de Beauvoir, *Faut-il brûler Sade?* (Paris, 1955), p. 20.

5. Didier, preface to *Aline et Valcour*, p. 18.

6. Jean Rousset, *Forme et Signification* (Paris, 1962). See especially chap. 4, "Une Forme littéraire: le roman par lettres."

7. One account of Sade's abilities as a letter novelist is that of Joseph Sexton, "Sade as an Epistolary Novelist," in *Les Bonnes Feuilles* (Penn State University) 3 [1974]:13–26. Sexton's conclusion is that Sade's letters in *Aline et Valcour* are purposely artificial to the extent that artifice itself triumphs in the end.

8. Letter from Mme. de Sade of June 1789, in *Oeuvres complètes*, 2:488–89.

9. Another example of Sade's use of Voltairian themes is the incident where Sainville rescues a woman forced into service as a beast of burden. When the rescue is completed, Sainville realizes that he had violated the local customs of Tamoé (4:240).

10. Béatrice Fink. "Ambivalence in the Gynogram: Sade's Utopian Woman," *Women and Literature* 7, no. 1 (1979):34.

11. Daniel Mornet, *La Pensée française au XVIIIe siècle* (Paris, 1965), p. 12.

12. Georges May, *Le Dilemme du roman au XVIIIe siècle* (Paris, 1963).

13. Roger Laufer, *Style rococo, style des lumières* (Paris: Corti, 1963), p. 19.

14. "L'Idée sur les romans" is published in Sade's *Oeuvres complètes*, 10:3–22. For an account of the evolution of this document, see Heine, "La Conception romanesque chez le Marquis de Sade," in *Le Marquis de Sade*, 286–98.

15. For additional illustrations of the contradictory practice of authorship of prose fiction and denunciation thereof in eighteenth-century France, see Lawrence W. Lynch, *Eighteenth-Century French Novelists and the Novel* (York, S.C.: French Literature Publications, 1979).

16. According to etymological dictionaries, the term *roman* derived from the vulgar Latin word *romanice,* meaning "in the manner of the Romans." It was also used to refer to a work written in vulgar Latin. The form which occurs at the time of Chrétien de Troyes is *romanz,* meaning a work in the vernacular (whether rhymed or in prose), and this form, together with the meaning of "romance," lingered until the distinctions made by writers such as Sade.

17. Rousseau, letter to Malesherbes of 22 August 1767.

18. Frédéric Deloffre, *Une Préciosité nouvelle: Marivaux et le marivaudage* (Paris: Colin, 1967).

19. Mornet, *La Pensée française,* p. 215.

20. Modern criticism has cast doubt on the accuracy of Sade's idea that Prévost translated Richardson's novels into French.

21. Lely, *Notice* to *Justine,* in *Oeuvres complètes,* 2:483–84.

22. See Lely's discussion of the problem in *Oeuvres complètes,* 2:594.

23. Laclos's aesthetic principles are quite close to those of Sade. He also cited the same models to be followed. See Lynch, "Laclos and Standards in Fiction," *Kentucky Romance Quarterly* 25, no. 2 (1978).

24. The original quotation is printed in Sade's *Oeuvres complètes,* 2:466–67.

25. Primary examples are Crébillon *fils,* preface to *Les Egarements du coeur et de l'esprit;* Diderot, *Eloge de Richardson;* Laclos, *De L'Education des femmes* and his review of Fanny Burney's *Cecilia.*

26. See bibliography.

Chapter Six

1. *La Marquise de Gange* is reproduced in volume 11 of Sade's *Oeuvres complètes.* Both *Isabelle de Bavière* and *Adelaïde de Brunswick* are found in volume 15.

2. *Oeuvres complètes,* 2:611.

3. *Faits des causes célèbres* (Amsterdam, 1757). This document is published as an appendix to *La Marquise de Gange,* in *Oeuvres complètes,* vol. 11.

4. As additional proof of the clarity in Sade's thinking between history and chronicle, we should observe that he cited the critic Huet, who also made the distinction (10:5). Georges May treats the relationship between history and fiction in "L'Histoire a-t-elle engendré le roman?" *Revue de l'histoire littéraire en France* 55 (1955):155–76.

5. Klossowski, *Sade mon prochain,* quoted by A. Laborde in "Sade: *La Marquise de Gange,*" *Symposium,* Spring 1969, p. 40.

6. Michaud, *Biographie universelle,* 15:508.

7. Vincent Cronin, *Louis XIV* (London: Book Club Associates, 1969), p. 87.

8. Barbara Tuchman, *A Distant Mirror* (New York: Ballantine, 1978), pp. 504–5.

9. Jacques Bainville, *Histoire de France* (Paris: Gallimard, 1924), p. 96.

10. Jules Michelet, *History of France,* trans. G. H. Smith (New York: Appleton, 1864), vol. 2, bks. 7–9.

11. See Lely's *Notice* on *Isabelle de Bavière,* in *Oeuvres complètes,* 2:610.

12. The same lack of condemnation of Isabelle's behavior prevails in Froissart's *Chroniques,* Juvenal des Ursin's *Histoire de Charles VI, Roy de France,* and in the other historical sources mentioned earlier.

13. Edward A. Lucie-Smith, *Joan of Arc* (New York: Norton, 1976), pp. 40–41.

14. Sade, *Correspondance,* in *Oeuvres complètes,* 12:605.

15. Hayman, *De Sade,* p. 223.

16. See the *Notice* on *Adelaïde de Brunswick,* in *Nouvelle Biographie générale* (Paris: Didot, 1857), 1:267.

17. Pages 140 and 155 of the novel provide additional examples of this process.

18. Didier, *Sade,* pp. 123–24.

19. The collection *Historiettes, Contes et Fabliaux* is virtually empty of any detailed character portrayals of women.

20. See, for example, the portrait of Amélie de Sancerre in *Oeuvres complètes,* 10:402.

21. Didier, *Notice* to *La Marquise de Gange* (Paris: Librairie générale française, 1974), pp. 258–59.

22. The concept of "le procédé de la verrue" (literally, the method of the "wart") was identified by Georges May in *Quatre Visages de Denis Diderot* (Paris: Boivin, 1951), pp. 201–9.

23. Klossowski, *Sade mon prochain* (Paris, 1967), p. 97.

Chapter Seven

1. Claude Duchet, "L'Image de Sade à l'époque romantique," in the *Colloque d'Aix-en-Provence* volume devoted to Sade (Paris: Colin, 1968), pp. 219–40.

2. Ibid., p. 232.

3. Sade, *Notes littéraires,* in *Oeuvres complètes,* 15:28.

4. Duchet, "L'Image de Sade," pp. 222–23.

5. Ibid., pp. 236–37.

6. Ibid., p. 225.

7. John A. Cassidy, *Algernon C. Swinburne* (New York: Twayne Publishers, 1964), p. 77.

8. Jeremy Mitchell, "Swinburne—the Disappointed Protagonist," *Yale French Studies* 35 (1965):82–84.

9. Baudelaire, "Projets et Notes diverses," in *Oeuvres complètes* (Paris: Seuil, 1968), p. 705; see also Lester Crocker, "Sade and the *Fleurs du mal*," in *Nature and Culture*, pp. 398–429.

10. Apollinaire, "Le Divin Marquis," in *L'Oeuvre du Marquis de Sade, pages choisies* (Paris, 1909), p. 232.

11. Quoted by J. H. Matthews, "The Right Person for Surrealism," *Yale French Studies* 35 (1965):94–95.

12. Ibid., pp. 89–95.

13. Ibid., p. 89.

14. Hayman, *De Sade,* pp. 233–34.

15. Camus, "La Négation absolue," in *L'Homme révolté* (Paris: Gallimard, 1965), p. 457.

16. Aldous Huxley, *Ends and Means* (New York: Harper & Row, 1937), pp. 313–14.

17. Alain Robbe-Grillet, preface to *La Nouvelle Justine,* and André Pieyre de Mandiargues, preface to *Juliette;* both essays are found in the Cercle précieux edition of Sade's *Oeuvres complètes.*

18. Beauvoir, *Faut-il brûler Sade?,* p. 14.

19. Klossowski, *Sade mon prochain.* The last point mentioned, that of *delectatio morosa,* was also treated in Klossowski's preface to Sade's *Crimes de l'amour (Oeuvres complètes,* vol. 10).

20. For a penetrating analysis of the interaction between these interpreters of Sade, see Gallop, *Intersections.*

21. Wallace Fowlie's *Lautréamont* (New York: Twayne Publishers, 1973) deals more directly with Sade's influence on Lautréamont. See particularly pp. 28–29, 108.

22. Laborde, *Sade romancier,* p. 107.

23. Didier, *Sade,* pp. 19–31.

24. This information was provided through the courtesy of the Archives service of Larousse and Cie.

25. The *Encyclopedia Britannica* has not displayed as much attitudinal progress, since it still refers to Sade as a "licentious" author.

26. Thomas, *The Marquis de Sade,* p. 153. See also *Oeuvres complètes,* 2:635.

27. Quoted by Gorer, *Marquis de Sade,* p. 16.

Selected Bibliography

PRIMARY SOURCES

Oeuvres complètes. Edited by Gilbert Lely. 16 vols. in 8. Tête de Feuilles
   edition. Paris: Gallimard, 1973. Same page and volume numbers
   as the Cercle du livre précieux edition of Sade's *Oeuvres complètes*
   (Paris: 1966–67).
Le Théâtre de Sade, Edited by Jean-Jacques Brochier. 4 vols. Paris:
   Pauvert, 1970.
The Marquis de Sade. Translated by Austryn Wainhouse and Richard
   Seaver. New York: Grove Press, 1965.

SECONDARY SOURCES

1.   Books
Apollinaire, Guillaume. *L'Oeuvre du Marquis de Sade, pages choisies.*
   Paris: Bibliothèque des curieux, 1909. A monumental date in the
   resurrection of Sade's writings at the beginning of this century.
Barthes, Roland. *Sade, Fourier, Loyola.* Translated by Richard Miller.
   New York: Hill & Wang, 1976. Contains two essays on Sade, one
   which stresses *imagination* as the key to Sadian *langage;* in the
   other, Sade is examined by a series of topics.
Beauvoir, Simone de. *Faut-il brûler Sade?* Paris: Gallimard, 1955. One
   of the most perspicacious essays written on Sade, by its superior
   account of his life, philosophy, and literary impact.
Blanchot, Maurice. *Lautréamont et Sade.* Paris: Editions de Minuit,
   1963. Not a comparative work, as the title might suggest, rather
   a brief structuralist interpretation of "la raison" of Sade.
Brooks, Peter. *The Novel of Worldliness.* Princeton: Princeton University
   Press, 1969. A reliable work on the evolution of the French novel,
   with emphasis on Crébillon, Marivaux, and Laclos.
Chanover, E. *The Marquis de Sade: A Bibliography.* Metuchen, N. J.:
   Scarecrow Press, 1973. Of the three or four bibliographies
   compiled on Sade between 1960 and 1980, this is the most
   complete.

Coulet, Henri. *Le Roman jusqu'à la Révolution.* Paris: Colin, 1967. A general introduction to the French novel.

Didier, Béatrice. *Sade: une écriture du désir.* Paris: Denoël-Gonthier, 1976. The most significant contribution of this series of essays is the identification of the *château intérieur* motif which permeates Sade's major works.

Gallop, Jane. *Intersections: A Reading of Sade with Bataille, Blanchot and Klossowski.* Lincoln: University of Nebraska Press, 1981. Assuming an "antihumanist" approach, the author provides interesting insights concerning the practices of the three major contributors to Sade studies, as well as her own account of pleasure, identity, and desire in Sade.

Gorer, Geoffrey. *The Life and Ideas of the Marquis de Sade.* New York: Norton, 1962. Places too much emphasis on Sade's political writings, and makes sweeping generalizations about his life and literary works.

Hayman, Ronald. *De Sade: A Critical Biography.* New York: Crowell, 1978. Although slightly digressive, one of the better English biographies of Sade.

Heine, Maurice. *Le Marquis de Sade.* Paris: Gallimard, 1950. Essays collected and published posthumously by Lely. Together with Lely's own work, this is one of the true pioneer works in Sade research.

Hénaff, Marcel. *Sade: l'Invention du corps libertin.* Paris: Presses universitaires de France, 1978. Difficult to read, sometimes unnecessarily obscure, but contains some very profound observations regarding *Les 120 Journées de Sodome* and the mechanical aspect of Sadian sexuality.

Klossowski, Pierre. *Sade mon prochain.* 1947. Reprint. Paris: Seuil, 1967. This provocative essay analyzes the relationship between Sadian eroticism and the reader, and ties the master-servant situation found in Sade to the deteriorating social conditions of late eighteenth-century France.

Laborde, Alice. *Sade romancier.* Neuchâtel: La Baconnière, 1974. The third chapter, which traces the evolution of the three forms of *Justine,* is the most important contribution to Sade exegesis.

Lacombe, Roger. *Sade et ses masques.* Paris: Payot, 1974. An interesting attempt at decoding Sade. Some conclusions regarding politics are specious, but the final part ("Sade historien du libertinage de son temps") is superior.

May, Georges. *Le Dilemme du roman au XVIIIᵉ siècle.* Paris: Presses universitaires de France, 1963. In spite of its date, this work remains the most complete and the most profound general analysis of the moral and aesthetic situation of prose fiction in eighteenth-century France.

Mornet, Daniel. *La Pensée française au XVIIIe siècle.* Paris: Colin, 1965. An indispensable introduction to the writings and thought of the major figures of the Enlightenment.

Rousset, Jean. *Forme et signification.* Paris: Corti, 1962. A remarkable series of essays on French literary form from Corneille to Claudel, and excellent in its exploration of the nature and potential of the epistolary novel.

Sgard, Jean. *Prévost romancier.* Paris: Corti, 1958. Using the multitude of Prévost's novels, this work is a complete account of the development of the memoir and historical forms of fiction.

Showalter, English. *The Evolution of the French Novel, 1641–1789.* Princeton: Princeton University Press, 1972. Concentrates on Challe and his *Illustres Françaises* as proof that most of the principal literary devices used by novelists were in place as early as 1713.

Stewart, Philip. *Imitation and Illusion in the French Memoir Novel, 1700–1750.* New Haven: Yale University Press, 1969. Incorporates minor authors with the major ones (primarily Prévost and Marivaux) in its discussion of their efforts to render their fictions credible.

Thomas, Donald. *The Marquis de Sade.* Boston: New York Graphic Society, 1976. A readable and generally accurate biography of Sade; suffers slightly from the omission of most of the French contributions to Sade.

2.   Articles

Barthes, Roland. "L'Arbre du crime." *Tel quel* 28 (Winter 1967):23–37. Using the concrete aspects of Sade's descriptive passages (food, clothing, physical appearance) Barthes demonstrates the rigidity and strict orchestration of Sadian society.

Delon, Michel. "Dix Ans d'études sadiennes, 1968–1978." *Dix-huitième Siècle: l'année 1778,* 1979. A valuable annotated bibliography of contributions to recent Sade studies.

Fink, Béatrice. "Ambivalence in the Gynogram: Sade's Utopian Woman." *Women and Literature* 7, no. 1 (1979):24–37. Shows that even in Sade's utopia (the Tamoé episode in *Aline et Valcour*), equality of the sexes is far from reality.

Lacan, Jacques. "Kant avec Sade." *Critique* 191 (April 1963):291–313. A monument of structuralist psychological interpretation of Sade which uses the pamphlet "Français, encore un effort . . ." to trace the role of the *fantasme* ("dream image") in the relationship between subject and object.

Lee, Vera. "The Sade Machine." *Studies on Voltaire and the Eighteenth Century* 98 (1972):207–18. The "machine" in question is Sade's "systematic oscillation between orgy and philosophy, cure and catastrophe."

Miller, Nancy. "*Justine,* or the Vicious Circle." *Studies in Eighteenth-Century Culture* 5 (1976):215–28. Based on analogies with *Candide* and other major works of the period, this essay shows the implausibility of Sade's descriptions of women.

Sollers, Philippe. "Sade dans le texte." *Tel Quel* 28 (Winter 1967):38–50. Another structuralist interpretation of Sade, which should be read with Barthes's contributions, and which argues that the perfect Sadian crime was that of "l'écriture."

Index

148